Who Is This Jesus Christ?

The Power of The Cross

Who Is This Jesus Christ?

The Power of The Cross

Dr. Finnian Ebuehi

ARPress
45 Dan Road Suite 15
Canton MA 02021
  Hotline: 1(888) 821-0229
  Fax: 1(508) 545-7580

Ordering Information:
Quantity sales. Special discounts are available on quantity purchases by corporations, associations, and others. For details, contact the publisher at the address above.

Printed in the United States of America.

ISBN-13:   Softcover   979-8-89676-479-3
             eBook   979-8-89676-480-9

Library of Congress Control Number: 2026906388

ABOUT THE AUTHOR

DR. FINNIAN EBUEHI

BIOGRAPHY

Finnian "Finn." Osak. Ebuehi is a Missionary Strategist, and Researcher. He is also a Professional Engineer, Social Worker, Clinical Therapist, and a Church Planter. Dr. Ebuehi studied from various continents: Africa, Asia, Europe, South and North America. He holds a bachelor's degree in mechanical engineering, a master's in divinity, a master's degree in Marriage and Family Therapy, and a Doctorate degree in Ministry.

He is the President and Co-founder of Christ's Harvesters Churches Ministries which is involved in strategic inreaches, outreaches/missions through Church Advancements/Planting, Discipleship, Leadership, Educational, and Infrastructural Developments in the most vulnerable nations of the globe

DEDICATION

The dedication of Who Is This Jesus Christ? The Power of The Cross book is foremost to the Blessed Trinity. God, the Father. God, the Son. God, the Spirit.

Though gone to Glory, this book is dedicated to each of these brethren who walked with The Holy Spirit :

JOE SALINAS,
COL.(RTD.) HENRY LADELE,
DR.ALBERT&MODUPE EHIOZUWA,
ADE. OGUNBOWALE,
EVANG. JEROME,
RACHEL ADEOYE,
DR. AARON TSADO,
ELIZABETH ADENOWO, AISOSA
GIDEON EBUEHI,
MAMA TOLIVER,
DR. WHALEN JONES, DEACON SAM. OMOTOSHO,
DEACON ERNEST WEBB.
ADDITIONALLY, THIS BOOK IS DEDICATED TO:
BOB PEARSON,
HELEN KUEKL,
DR. ELIZABETH EBUEHI, MY BELOVED WIFE,
BRETHREN IN AGAPE CHRISTIAN CHURCH,
GOOD SHEPHERD CHURCH,
EXALTED WORD CHURCH,
ST. STEPHENS BAPTIST CHURCH,
ST. STEPHENS BAPTIST CHURCH,
MESSIAH BAPTIST CHURCH,
CHRIST'S HARVESTERS CHURCHES MINISTRIES,
EMMANUAL ANDE,
NASARA BAPTIST CHURCH, CAPRO, CMF,
OPEN CHRISTIAN FELLOWSHIP,
U.U. NTA, O.J. OGBUOJI, JIMMY ZELLNER,
AND TO YOU.

CONTENTS

PREFACE

I love Jesus as a Person, as my Lord, Advocate, and Friend. Jesus is everything to me. He's the "historical Jesus," yes, a human as He appeared on earth and walked the dusty roads of Galilee. But He is much more. He was with God at the beginning. All things were made through Him. He is the Redeemer of mankind, the Shepherd of souls. He is the One by whom all will be judged. And He is the Perfectly Perfect who will wrap up the world and make it a place where, once more, righteousness dwells. He is God the Son.

"He came to his own, and his own received him not…" John 1:11.

"Yet to all who receive him, to those who believed in his name, he gave the right to become children of God." John 1:12.

I'd like to explore with you the various facets of Jesus' person, life, and mission. One way to do this is by carefully studying the Gospels and Epistles. But another way is to approach it topically–by Jesus' names, titles, descriptors and the metaphors. The Gospel of John's opening passages describes Jesus as God incarnate and the reality that the Holy Scriptures story point to. The first chapter of John introduces Jesus as the Word from the Greek logos and clearly describes Jesus as God. *This book – Who Is This Jesus Christ? The Power of The Cross* was written a long time ago in a different language and in culture very different from the modern/contemporary Western world. Jesus probably spoke in Aramaic language, but the New

Testament was originally written in Greek. The styles of writing, nuances of the language and figures of speech as nonfamiliar to modern readers. No translation into English can fully capture the riches and details of the original writings— to truly understand Jesus' teachings we need to understand the background life, and literature in the first century A.D. as the Gospel being written. The real goals of the Holy Spirit interpretation are to understand the author's originally intended meaning and lives as it was understood by the original audience. Then we can better understand, and the principles Jesus taught concerning life in the present digital world.

The biblical narratives contain details that you probably have not noticed before. These details reflect historical realities you probably did not know before. These insights will challenge you to love Jesus more and to serve HIM more. I'll try to mention at least once all these names, titles, descriptors, and metaphors. But I'll concentrate on the ones most used in Holy Scripture. If you understand Jesus in these chief names and titles, then the seldom used, but precious names will be icing on the cake for you.

What we're about to commence on is actually "theology"—the study of God.

Of course, there'll be some overlap and repetition, since these names and themes are interwoven, with several often mentioned in the same passage. But that's fine. We're going swimming together, and though we'll try to keep the study organized, the most important thing is to enjoy the water.

I don't want this to be merely academic or head knowledge. My goal doing this study is to help you enter a deeper relationship with Jesus.

CHAPTER 1A
THE SIGNIFICANCE OF HIS DEATH.

Holy Scriptures Text: John 19:16-37

In this study, we are to consider what to every Bible-loving, born again, saved person is the most precious of all themes – the death of our Lord and Savior Jesus Christ; and we are to pay particular attention to the unique nature and the special significance of His death. That His death is an historic fact; but there are many views, ideas, interpretations and theories as to why He died, and yet how wonderfully explicit the scriptures are! We cannot pretend to comprehend fully the deep significance of the death of the Lord Jesus upon Calvary's cross, but we can believe that He died for us, and we can rejoice in the blessings which are ours by virtue of that unique and saving death. One verse of one of our most popular hymns is helpful in this connection.

Meditate upon it:

"He died so that we might be forgiven, … This gives us PARDON for the past.

He died to make us good; … This gives us POWER for the present.

That we might go at last to Heaven…This gives us PROSPECT for the future

Saved by His precious blood." Look up 1 Peter 1:17-21.

This is deep theology, and yet it is so simple and clear that even a child can understand the fact that our Lord Jesus Christ died and shed His precious blood to save us all. Look up and prayerfully study the following references:

(1) Isaiah 53:5-6.

(2) John 1:29.

(3) John 3:14.

(4) John 10:18.

(5) Romans 5:6,10

(6) 1 Corinthians 15:3.

(7) 2 Corinthians 5:21.

(8) Galatians 3:13.

(9) Hebrews 9:26.

(10) 1 Peter 3:18.

These scriptures (and many others) summarize the teaching of the Word of God concerning the death of the Lord Jesus; and it is clear from these references that His death was unique and that it was deeply significant. Now notice the following:

The death of the Lord Jesus was:

(1)Predetermined in eternity – look up Acts 4:26-28.

(2)1 Peter 1:19-20 and Revelation 13:8.
(2) Predicted in the Old Testament – look up Genesis 3:15; Isaiah 53; Luke 24:25-27 and Acts 10:43.
(3) Pictured in the types – look up Genesis 22 and Exodus 12.
(4) Prominent in the Gospels – look up Matthew 27:45-50; Mark 15:33-41; Luke 23:44-49 and John 19:30-37.
(5) Predominant in the Epistles – look up Romans 5:6; 1 Corinthians 1:23; Galatians 1:4; Hebrews 9:26 and 1 Peter 2:21-24.
(6) The Principal Theme in Heaven – look up Revelation 1:5-7 and Revelation 5:6-12.
(7) The Permanent Theme-song of the ages – look up Revelation 5:9-12.

But let us ask the all-important question: Why did the Lord Jesus die? This must be answered negatively and positively.

Negatively:

(1) He did not die a suicide's death – look up Isaiah 53:8.
(2) He did not die of old age, accident or disease – look up John 10:18.
(3) He did not die as a political hero – look up Luke 24:21.
(4) He did not die simply as an example – look up John 15:13.
(5) He did not die simply as a martyr – look up Acts 7:54-60.
(6) He did not die simply to show God's love – look up Romans 5:8.
(7) He did not die because He was a criminal – look up Luke 23:4.

Positively:

Here are five very important truths in connection with our Savior's death:

1. The Lord Jesus came into the world to die

His death was a necessity (Hebrews 9:22). Moreover, He knew He had come to die (Matthew 16:21; Matthew 17:12; Luke 9:51; John 3:14, and John 10:11). These scriptures make this quite clear. He was not, as has been blasphemously suggested, 'surprised and disappointed when He found He must die!' It was planned in the eternity past that He should come into the world to die for us – look up Revelation 13:8 again!

2. The Lord Jesus died willingly, voluntarily.

As the sinless One, there was no cause of death in Himself. See what John 10:18 and Matthew 26:53 say. See also Psalm 40:8; Mark 14:41; Luke 22:53; John 7:30 and John 8:20. He voluntarily laid down His life for us because it was the will of His Father that He should do so and because He loved us so much!

3. The Lord Jesus died as a sacrifice for sin, to put away sin.

How clear the scriptures are! Look up and meditate upon Isaiah 53:5-6; John 1:29; 1 Corinthians 15:3; 2 Corinthians 5:21; Hebrews 9:26 and 1 Peter 2:24.

Why did He die? He died to put away sin by the sacrifice of Himself.

4. The Lord Jesus died as our Substitute, bearing our penalty

Yes, "we believe it was for us. He hung and suffered there". He died instead of us, in our place, and He bore the punishment which was due to us – look up Isaiah 53:5; John 10:11 and 1 Peter 3:18.

Thus we see why God has not dealt with us after our sins (Psalm 103:10). He has fully, finally and justly dealt with our sin (and our sins) in the Person and through the sacrificial death of His Son. So, the innocent victim took the place of the guilty sinner and bore away his sin in His body on the tree (1 Peter 2:24). It is by believing this great fact – look up Acts 16:30-31; and accepting this loving Savior – look up John 1:12; that I am saved and able to say, 'He loved me, and gave Himself for me' – look up Galatians 2:20.

5. The Death of the Lord Jesus was victorious.

At Calvary He provided salvation for all mankind – look up John 3:16 and 1 John 2:2. His death is sufficient for all, but it is efficient only for those who believe. His death was victorious in that He rose again, and thereby demonstrated that all the claims of divine justice had been met by His death and that salvation had been procured for all who would believe – look up John 9:35.

Do you believe it? Can you say, "It is enough that Jesus died, and that He died for me?"

CHAPTER 1B
THE SIGNIFICANCE OF JESUS CHRIST.

The Significance of the Death of Christ Jesus.
Wrong Views of the Significance
of the Death of Jesus
The Governmental View

This view suggests that Jesus died to show us the strong displeasure of God towards sin. While it is true that His death shows us the strong displeasure of God towards sin, this view fails by teaching that the death of Jesus served merely as an alternative to your punishment. By teaching that His death was similar or comparable to the death that you deserve, it fails to recognize that He died the exact and complete death that you deserve. As such, this view presents the death of Jesus as a technical necessity rather than an actual fulfillment of the punishment your sin deserves. Furthermore, it diminishes the significance of the death of Jesus.

The Moral Influence View

This view suggests that Jesus died to show His incomparable love for sinful people and to inspire you to turn from your sin to God. While it is true that His death reveals the magnificent love of God towards sinners, this view falls short by teaching that His death was nothing more than a demonstration of love, a most extravagant display of divine love (John 3:16; Rom 5:8).

But Jesus did not die merely to demonstrate His love; He died to accomplish something more significant. Furthermore, He did not attempt merely to motivate you to turn from your sins. After all, nothing in the world – not even the most supreme act of love – is able to persuade you emotionally to turn from your sin (John 3:19). Jesus died to accomplish something more significant and certain.

The Example View

This view suggests that Jesus died to provide you with an example of true obedience and to inspire you to live in a similar way. While it is true that Jesus intends for anyone who believes on Him for salvation to follow Him through suffering, this view falls short by teaching that the death of Jesus was merely an example of obedience to follow (1 Pet 2:21). Jesus died to accomplish something more, something that not only inspires and instructs you to do good, but also enables you to do so for real. Furthermore, this view disregards the need for personal repentance and salvation by teaching that anyone may aspire to be like Jesus through noble effort and good deeds.

The Accident View

This view suggests that Jesus died as a result of overconfidence about His identity and mission. While the three views previously mentioned fail by providing an incomplete perspective, this view fails entirely. The death of Jesus was not an unfortunate event which He could have avoided. He did not die because His claims to be the Messiah somehow "got to His head" and caused Him to "go too far" and to "take on more than He could handle." Instead, Jesus taught beforehand that He would die (Matt 16:21; 17:22). His death was no surprise. He intended to die. In fact, His death was an eternal and intentional feature in the plan of God (Acts 2:23). Furthermore, by claiming to be God and Messiah, Jesus did not claim too much. He spoke the truth.

The Martyr View

This view suggests that Jesus died because He threatened the status quo with His radical ideas. Though Jesus did threaten the status quo, His primary antagonists merely lobbied for the Roman government to execute Him on these grounds – that He was a political threat to Rome. However, they wanted Him executed for a different and deeper reason, namely that He claimed to be the Son of God. Knowing this, the martyr view fails to recognize the underlying spiritual significance of the death of Jesus (John 10:33).

A Correct View of the Significance of the Death of Jesus

Substitution

When Jesus died, He did something very significant. He died to take your place. He stood where you deserve to stand. He hung where you deserve to hang. He died the death that you deserve to die. He fully, personally, and directly received on Himself the punishment that you rightly deserve to receive for your own sins. But instead of you receiving this punishment for yourself, Jesus became your substitute. He took your place.

He received on Him the punishment that you deserve.

Paul alludes to this when he wrote, "He made him who knew no sin to be sin for us, that we might become the righteousness of God in Him (2 Cor 5:21)."

The little English word for in the phrase "sin for us" is used for a Greek word which means "in the place of." You could read this verse in this way, "He made him who knew no sin to be sin in our place."

In another place, Paul uses this word when he says, "Christ has redeemed us from the curse of the law, having become a curse for us" (Gal 3:13).

The word for reflects the same Greek word meaning "in the place of."

The idea is this: Jesus died on the cross in the place of you, because you needed to die for your sins, but you were not able to do so in a satisfactory way. So, Jesus stepped in under the punishment that you deserve, and He let your punishment fall on Him in your place.

Redemption

When Paul described the death of Jesus in substitutionary terms, he also taught another aspect of the significance of the death of Jesus – redemption.

He said, "Christ has redeemed us from the curse of the law, having become a curse for us" (Gal 3:13). Redemption means "to release from slavery by the payment of a price."

To what were you enslaved? You were enslaved by the curse of the law, an empty lifestyle, and all kinds of iniquity (Gal 3:13; 1 Pet 1:18; Tit 2:14; Heb 2:14-15). You were enslaved to sin. Sin was your master. You had to sin. You were unable to do otherwise.

Jesus died to liberate you from this enslavement to sin.

What was the price for your freedom?

Peter teaches, "You were not redeemed with corruptible things, like silver or gold, from your aimless conduct received by tradition from your fathers, but with the precious blood of Christ" (Eph 1:7; 1 Pet 1:18-19). Jesus paid the most expensive price. Nothing is more precious or priceless than this.

For what were you redeemed? You were redeemed so that you would do good works, the kind which are genuinely good (Titus 2:14). Furthermore, you were redeemed so that you would someday be received into the family of God for eternity as a child of God. The Bible calls this "the adoption of sons" (Gal 4:5). Ultimately, you have been redeemed, liberated and purchased out from the slave market of sin so that you will glorify and serve the God who loves you (1 Cor 6:20; 7:23).

Propitiation

Jesus not only died to be your substitute and to redeem you from enslavement to sin (and the consequences of sin). He also died to appease God's wrath towards sinners, including you. John tells us, "He himself is the propitiation for our sins" (1 John 2:2). Propitiation is an important theological and doctrinal word. It means "to satisfy the wrath of another person by means of an offering or a gift."

Some people claim that God cannot be angry because He is a loving God. However, anyone who loves deeply also knows what it means to be angry. Just as goodness elicits joy and true delight, that which is evil elicits deep displeasure and anger.

Therefore, the God who loves perfectly also displays

anger in its strongest form. Scripture teaches that our loving God is angry with sinners every day (Psalms 7:11), though He certainly loves them at the same time (John 3:16).

Knowing this, it is most remarkable to understand that the death of Jesus reveals to us the incredible love of God, even with reference to His wrath towards sinners. True stories may be told of people inhabiting jungles and mountains who seek to appease the wrath of their false gods, demons and deceased ancestors. To appease this wrath, they do ridiculous things. They walk on hot coals and climb ladders made of knives. They destroy neighboring villages. They offer their children as human sacrifices. Yet by doing all these things and more, they can never satisfy the anger that they feel is upon them.

The death of Jesus shows that the one true God is different. Though he is deeply, genuinely and perfectly angry towards sinners, He does not expect you, nor I, nor anyone else to resolve His anger towards our sin. Knowing that we are unable to do so, He took upon himself the sin and punishment that we all deserve. Jesus, who is God, allowed the wrath of God for your sin and mine to fall upon Himself instead. In this way, He maintained the justice that is necessary while also being merciful. In this way also, as in so many others, God is unlike the false religions of the world.

Of Jesus, Paul says this: "Whom God set forth as a propitiation by his blood, through faith, to demonstrate his righteousness … that he might be just and the justifier of the one who has faith in Jesus" (Rom 3:25-26). He not only judges your sin, but He judges your sin by taking your place and pouring out His anger on Himself, on Jesus Christ.

Reconciliation

Jesus died to restore peace between God and sinners. Paul describes this concept in this way:

"All things are of God, who hath reconciled us to himself by Jesus Christ, and hath given to us the ministry of reconciliation" (2 Cor 5:18).

Reconciliation means "to restore peace between two opposing, hostile parties." By nature, every person is hostile towards God. But your hostility to God is unlike the kind that often exists between two people or two groups of people.

When two people or groups of people are at odds with one another, they both carry a percentage of blame. Both contribute their own sinfulness to the broken relationship, but in your relationship to God, you are the only party who contributes to the brokenness. Just like Adam and Eve in the beginning, you walked away from God. You resisted and rebelled against the good, loving, and perfect will and design of God for your life.

Since this is the case, you would think that God expects you to make things right. You would think that God expects you to take steps to reverse your rebellion and correct your sin, but such is not the case. That's why Paul says, "All things are of God, who hath reconciled us to himself by Jesus Christ, and hath given to us the ministry of reconciliation" (2 Cor 5:18).

All things are of God because through the death of Jesus, God does "all the things" that are necessary to restore your relationship to Him, even though you are the one who walked away.

In a normal reconciliation, both sides must recognize where they have spoken and acted in a wrongful manner.

They must say things, do things and offer things as a gift to remove hostility and restore peace in the relationship. But through the death of Jesus, God has provided the necessary gift on your behalf to restore your relationship to Him forever. In this way, the reconciliation of the cross is more remarkable indeed.

REFLECTIONS:

You deserve to die, but Jesus died in your place.

You were in bondage to sin, but Jesus made you free.

You deserved God's wrath, but Jesus appeased this wrath.

You were separated from God, but Jesus restored this relationship.

CHAPTER 2
THE POWER OF THE CROSS.

SALIENT AREAS TO NOTE ON THE CROSS OF JESUS CHRIST.

1. The Cross is a Trinitarian event.

The Christian faith is distinctively Trinitarian and cross-shaped. Therefore, the cross must reveal the Trinity. God the Father sent the Son to save the world, the Son submitted to the Father's will, and the Spirit applies the work of redemption to Jesus followers. Redemption is predestined by the Father (Eph 1:3–6), accomplished by the Son (Eph 1:7–10), and applied by the Spirit (Eph. 1:13–14). God did not withhold the Son, and the Son surrendered to the Father. Yet the father is not only sacrificing the Son. The Father, the Son, and the Spirit all possess a single will. The sacrifice, while uniquely the Son's work, is also the will of the three persons.

2. The Cross is the center of the story of the Scripture.

A Bible without a cross is a Bible without a climax, a Bible without an ending, a Bible without a solution. The spiral of sin that began in Genesis 3 must be stopped; the death of Jesus terminates the downward spiral. In Jesus's body, he took on the sin of the world and paid the price of all humanity.

At the cross the new Adam, Abraham, Moses, David arises to create a new humanity, family, and kingdom. That is why Paul doesn't say he decided to be knowing nothing except the incarnation, resurrection, or the ascension of Jesus, but the nothing except Jesus Christ and him crucified (1 Cor. 2:2). Wisdom was found not beyond the cross, not above the cross, not below the cross, but in the cross.

3. The Cross redefines power in the kingdom.

Jesus's announcement that the kingdom of God has come is conclusively revealed in the Christ-event on the cross. The Scriptures narrate how God will manifest his kingship on the earth. He gives Adam and Eve the task of ruling and reigning over the earth as his representatives, but they attempt to seize power for themselves (Gen. 3:5). In fact, all their children do the same. Babel (or Babylon) is the city opposed to the reign of God. Jesus comes as the true Son and redefines power by displaying strength through weakness. He does not exploit his power like Adam but empties himself (Phil. 2:5–6).

He becomes a servant of all, and thereby is exalted as ruler of all (Phil. 2:9–11).

4. The Cross inaugurates the new covenant.

At the Last Supper Jesus interprets his death as bringing in the new covenant. It is by his body and blood that his new community is formed. Just as the people of Israel were sprinkled with blood as they entered a covenant with Yahweh, so the disciples are members of the new community by the pouring out of Jesus's blood. The new covenant community now has the Torah written on their hearts and they all know the Lord because of the gift of the Spirit (Jer. 31:33–34).

The Cross is not only where our sin is paid for, where the devil is conquered, but the shape of Christianity.

5. The Cross conquers sin and death.

The cross cancels the record of debt that stood against humanity (Col 2:14). On the cross Jesus bore our sins in his body, so that we might die to sin and death (1 Pet. 2:24). The curse of sin and death was placed on Jesus so that we might obtain the blessings of Abraham (Gal 3:13). Understanding the cross and resurrection as a single event is important here, for it is through the death and resurrection of Christ that death is swallowed up in victory (1 Cor. 15:54–55).

6. The Cross vanquishes the devil.

On the cross, Christ did not only conquer sin and death, but he conquered the spiritual forces of darkness. A cosmic eruption occurred at Golgotha; a new apocalyptic force entered the world, and the old magic was conquered by a deeper magic. He disarmed the power and authorities, putting them to open shame, and triumphs over them on the cross (Col. 2:14). When Christ rises from the dead he is seated at the right hand of the Father in the heavenly places, far above all rule and authority and power (Eph. 2:20–21).

7. The Cross is substitutionary.
The cross is for us, in our place, on our behalf.

He laid down his life for His sheep.

He is our sacrificial lamb. "Behold the Lamb of God who takes away the sin of the world" (John 1:29). Just as Abraham raised his eyes and looked and saw a ram to offer as a burnt offering in the place of his son (Gen 22:13), so too we look up and see Jesus as our replacement. He became a curse for us (Gal 3:13), meaning he takes the place of all the enslaved, the rebels, the idolaters, and the murderers. If the conquering of the spiritual forces is the goal, then substitution is the ground or basis for this conquering (Gal. 1:4).

"The cross represents not only the great exchange (substitutionary atonement), but also the great transition (the eschatological turn of the ages)."

The Kingdom of God and the Glory of the Cross

Patrick Schreiner

Defining the kingdom of God as the interplay of the king's power over the king's people in the king's place, this volume helps readers understand God's purpose for the world.

8. The Cross is foolishness to the world.

In a PBS television series, the narrator said, "Christianity is the only major religion to have as its central focus the suffering and degradation of its God." And Paul acknowledges that this message of Christ crucified will be a stumbling block to Jews and folly to Gentiles (1 Cor 1:23).

It is not an inherently attractive message, until spiritual

eyes of sight are granted.

The world looks at the cross and sees weakness, irrationality, hate, and disgust. In the early decades of the Christian movement the scandal of the cross was most self-evident thing about it. It was not only the death of the Messiah, but the manner of his death that is an offense.

9. The Cross brings peace, reconciliation, and unity.

At the cross the whole world can be reconciled to the Father. The peace that the world has been seeking, the unity of all people is found in blood. "For he himself is our peace, who has made us both one and has broken down in his flesh the dividing wall of hostility" (Eph. 2:14). Reconciliation for the world, peace, shalom, and unity comes only by the blood of the cross (Col 1:20). No blood means no harmony.

10. The Cross is the marching order for Christians.

After Jesus explained to his disciples that he must suffer, he tells them, "If anyone would come after me, let him deny himself and take up his cross and follow me" (Matt 16:24).

Paul embodies the cross in his ministry, becoming the fragrance of death as he is lead on the triumphal procession (2 Cor. 2:14–17), and he evens says he has been crucified with Christ (Gal 2:20). But Paul does not merely apply the cross to his own ministry, but he instructs the new community at Philippi to have the mind of Christ (Phil. 2:5) which is defined by Jesus's humility on the cross (Phil. 2:8).

The cross is not only where our sin is paid for, where

the devil is conquered, but the shape of Christianity.

As Rutledge has said, "the crucifixion is the touchstone of Christian authenticity, the unique feature by which everything else. . . is given true significance."

CHAPTER 3

THE ISLAMIC PERSPECTIVES AND APOLOGETICS.

CLICHÉ OF GOD IN ISLAM AND CHRISTIANITY.

My major interaction with Islam was ushered in my life with my mandatory national service to Borno State in the Northeast of Nigeria. It is worth noting that the genesis of Borko Haram was from the Northeast of that country. After the successful completion of my one year national service, by God divine direction, I was employed as a pioneer Maintenance Engineer to work with a wonderful group of European Expatriates and Engineers for the establishment of the first ever meter/circuit breaker manufacturing plant in the south of the Sahara/North Africa. The technical partners were Landis & GYR, Switzerland., which was later taken over by Siemens, of Germany. With the local exposure to the Muslims, my interest in Islam was quickened by my study of the history of the cosmological argument for a personal creator of the universe. Early Christian commentators on Aristotle living in Alexandria, Egypt, developed this argument in response to Aristotle's doctrine of the eternity of the world. They sought to show that the universe had a beginning and was brought into being by a transcendent creator.

When Islam swept across North Africa in the eighth century, this argument was taken up into Islamic theology and developed during the Middle Ages to a high degree of sophistication. Because of the contribution of Islamic thinkers to this argument, I dubbed it the kalam cosmological argument, the word "kalam" being the Arabic word for Islamic theology. I believe that this is a sound argument for God's existence, and it has served me well in reaching out to Muslims with the gospel.

With the attacks of 9/11, Islam suddenly burst into public consciousness in the West, and its profile has risen with each passing year, as Islamic terrorism has spread across the world. This heightened awareness of Islam has piqued people's interest in Islam and given me the opportunity to speak about the commonalities and contrasts between Islam and Christianity. Today I've been asked to speak about the concept of God in Islam and Christianity.

The question which drives our inquiry is not merely one of comparative religion; rather it is whether the Christian or Muslim concept of God is true. In our day of religious relativism, such a question is incredibly politically incorrect. All religions are supposed to be equally true, right? So, what's the fuss all about?

Well, the answer to that question, it seems to me, is that religious relativism, which is almost unthinkingly accepted by many people today, is simply not true. In fact, religious relativism is logically incoherent and so cannot be true. For the world's religions conceive of God, or gods, in so many contradictory ways that they cannot all be true. In particular, the concept of God in Islam and Christianity is so different that both religions cannot be right. Islam and Christianity have different doctrines or teachings concerning what God is like. For example, Christians believe that God is tri-personal, that there are in the one God three persons whom we call the Father, Son, and Holy

Spirit. Muslims deny this doctrine or teaching. They believe that God is a single person. We cannot both be right. We could both be wrong—maybe it's the Buddhists who are right and God is impersonal—but we cannot both be correct. Therefore, part of the job of evaluating the competing claims of Islam and Christianity will be assessing their differing concepts of God.

Accordingly, in this morning's talk I want, first, to look at the principal Islamic critique of the Christian conception of God, and then, second, to critically examine the Muslim concept of God, with a view toward determining its adequacy.

So, let's look first at the Christian concept of God and ask why Muslims find it rationally objectionable. Christians believe that God is an all-powerful, all-knowing, all-holy, eternal, spiritual Being who created the universe. Muslims agree with all these attributes (or properties) of God. This isn't surprising, since Islam, historically speaking, is an offshoot of the Judeo-Christian religious tradition. So, our understanding of what God is like is in many respects the same.

But the major objection lodged by Islam against the Christian concept of God concerns the doctrine of the Trinity. Christians believe that Jesus Christ is the Son of God and shares the same divine nature with God the Father. Muslims reject this doctrine because they believe that it commits the sin they call shirk, which is the sin of associating anything with God. Since God is thought to be incomparable or without peer, He cannot have a Son, as Christians claim. Thus, the Qu 'ran denounces anyone who holds that God has a Son as "an unbeliever" and consigns him to hellfire for such a blasphemous assertion.

The Qur'an states: "They are unbelievers who say, 'God

is the Messiah, Mary's son...' Surely, whoever associates anything with God, God shall prohibit his entrance to Paradise and his home shall be the Fire. None shall help the evildoers" (5.73).

Unfortunately, the Qur'an's denunciation of the doctrine of the Trinity seems to be based on a gross misunderstanding of that doctrine. First, a bit of history here: Early Christian creeds had adopted the language of speaking of Mary as "the mother of God" because she bore Jesus Christ. Now to someone not familiar with the theology of the early Church Fathers, such an expression as "the mother of God" is almost guaranteed to be misleading. What the Church Fathers meant is that the person whose human nature Mary bore is a divine person. Mary did not give birth to the divine nature of Christ; nevertheless, Mary could be called the Mother of God, since Christ, whose human nature she bore, was a divine person.

But Mohammed evidently thought that Christians believed in a Trinity composed of God the Father, Mary, and their offspring Jesus. It's no wonder that he regarded such a ridiculous doctrine as blasphemous! Mohammed's misunderstanding of the Trinity is evident in passages such as the following found in the Qur'an:

God will say: 'Jesus Son of Mary, did you ever say to mankind: "Worship me and my mother as gods besides God?"'

'Glory be to you,' he will answer, 'I could never have claimed what I have no right to.' (5.117)

The Creator of the heavens and the earth—how should he have a son, seeing that He has no consort, and He created all things . . . ? (6.102)

The doctrine that Mohammed rejected, namely, that

God the Father should consort with a human female to sire a son and these three should then be worshiped as gods, would be rejected by any Christian.

According to the Bible, Jesus is called God's Son because he had no human father but was miraculously conceived of a virgin. In the Gospel according to Luke, the angel says to Mary, "The Holy Spirit will come on you, and God's power will rest upon you. For this reason, the holy child will be called the Son of God" (Luke 1.35 TEV). What makes this ironic is that the Qur'an affirms the virgin birth of Jesus! In the Qur'anic account the angel says, "I am but a messenger of your Lord and have come to give you a holy son."

Mary answers, "How shall I bear a son when I have neither been touched by any man nor ever been unchaste?" The angel replies, "Thus did your Lord speak. That is easy enough for me . . . . Our decree shall come to pass." (19.20-22). Whereupon Mary conceived Jesus. Thus, no Muslim should object to calling Jesus God's Son in the sense of his being miraculously conceived.

So, if the doctrine of the Trinity is not the caricature rightly rejected by Mohammed, what is it? It is the doctrine that God is tri personal. It is not the self-contradictory assertion that three Gods are one God, nor again that three persons are one person. That's just illogical nonsense. Rather it is the claim that the one entity we call God comprises three persons. That is no more illogical than saying that one geometrical figure we call a triangle is comprised of three angles. Three angles in one figure; three persons in one being!

Perhaps the best way to think of this is to say that in God there are three centers of self-consciousness. I am a being with a single center of self-consciousness. God is a being with three centers of self-consciousness. Each of these three persons is equal in glory and divinity; but we call them "Father," "Son," and "Holy Spirit" because of the different roles they place in relation to us. The Father is the person who sends the Son to Earth; the Son is the person who takes a human nature and becomes incarnate as Jesus of Nazareth; the Holy Spirit is the person who stands in Christ's place until Christ returns.

Although this doctrine may seem strange to Muslims, once it's properly stated, there's nothing rationally objectionable about it. It is a logically consistent doctrine and seems rationally unobjectionable.

In fact, I'd like to finish out my first point by offering an argument for why it's plausible to think that God is a Trinity. To begin with, God is the greatest conceivable being. If you could conceive of anything greater than God, then that would be God! Every Muslim who dies with the cry "Allahu Akbar!" on his lips agrees with this point: God is the greatest being conceivable.

Now as the greatest conceivable being, God must be perfect. If there were any imperfection in God, then He would not be the greatest conceivable being. Now a perfect being must be a loving being. For love is a moral perfection; it is better for a person to be loving rather than unloving. God therefore must be a perfectly loving being.

Now it is of the very nature of love to give oneself away. Love reaches out to another person rather than centering wholly in oneself. So, if God is perfectly loving by His very nature, He must be giving Himself in love to another. But who is that other? It cannot be any created person, since creation is a result of God's free will, not a result of His nature. It belongs to God's very essence to love, but it does not belong to His essence to create anything. God is necessarily loving, but He is not necessarily creating. So, we can imagine a possible world in which God is perfectly loving and yet no created persons exist. So created persons cannot be the sufficient explanation of whom God loves. Moreover, science tells us that created persons have not always existed. But God is eternally loving. So again, created persons alone are insufficient to account for God's being perfectly loving. It therefore follows that the other to whom God's love is necessarily directed must be internal to God Himself.

In other words, God is not a single, isolated person, as Islam holds; rather God is a plurality of persons, as the Christian doctrine of the Trinity holds. On the Islamic view God is a person who does not give Himself away essentially in love for another; He is focused essentially only on Himself. Hence, He cannot be the most perfect being. But on the Christian view, God is a triad of persons in eternal, self-giving love relationships. Thus, since God is essentially loving, the doctrine of the Trinity is more plausible than any unitarian doctrine of God such as Islam. Why? Because God is by nature a perfect Being of self-giving love.

In summary of my first point, then, we've seen that the classic Muslim rejection of the Christian concept of God is based on a drastic misunderstanding of the doctrine of the Trinity, and that once that doctrine is properly understood, it is not only rationally unobjectionable, but quite plausible as well. Therefore, the Christian concept of God is rationally unobjectionable.

That brings us to my second point, that the Muslim concept of God is rationally objectionable. Now in claiming this, I'm not trying to put anybody down or attack someone personally. I'm just saying that it seems to me that the Islamic conception of God has real problems which render it rationally objectionable. Let me share just one of those deficits, namely:

Islam has a morally deficient concept of God.

We've seen that Muslims and Christians agree that God is the greatest conceivable being and that besides being all-powerful, all-knowing, all-present, and so forth, the greatest conceivable being must also be morally perfect. That means that God must be a loving and gracious being. Therefore, God, as the perfect being, must be all-loving.

And this is exactly what the Bible affirms. The Bible says, God is love, . . . In this is love, not that we loved God but that He loved us and sent His son to be the sacrifice for our sins (I John 4.8, 10).

Or again it says, God shows His love for us in that while we were, yet sinners Christ died for us (Romans 5.8).

Jesus taught God's unconditional love for sinners. We see this in his parables about the prodigal son and the lost sheep, in his practice of table fellowship with the immoral and unclean, and in his sayings like those of the Sermon on the Mount. He said, for example, you have heard that it was said, 'You shall love your neighbor and hate your enemy.' But I say to you, love your enemies and pray for those who persecute you, so that you may be sons of your Father who is in heaven; for He makes His sun rise on the evil and on the good, and sends his rain on the just and on the unjust. For if you love those who love you, . . . what more are you doing than others? Do not even the Gentiles do the same? You therefore must be perfect, as your heavenly Father is perfect. (Matthew 5.43-48)

The love of the Heavenly Father is impartial, universal, and unconditional.

What a contrast with the God of the Quran! What I'm

going to tell you now is something that you will never hear in the media or from our public officials, for they dare not say such things. They cannot risk alienating hundreds of millions of Muslims by saying anything critical of Islam. But honesty compels me to say candidly and without rancor that the God of the Qur'an is not the loving God revealed by Jesus. According to the Quran, God does not love sinners. This fact is emphasized repeatedly and consistently like a drumbeat throughout the pages of the Qur'an. Just listen to the following passages:

"God loves not the unbelievers" (III.33)

"God loves not the impious and sinners"(II.277)

"God loves not evildoers" (III. 58)

"God loves not the proud" (IV. 37)

"God loves not transgressors" (V. 88)

"God loves not the prodigal" (VI. 142)

"God loves not the treacherous" (VIII.59)

"God is an enemy to unbelievers" (II. 99)

Repeatedly the Qur'an declares that God does not love the very people whom the Bible says God loves so much that He sent His Son to die for them!

Now this may seem paradoxical considering the Qur'an's calling God "al-Rahman al-Rahim" –the All-Merciful—until you realize that according to the Qur'an what God's mercy really cashes out to is that if you believe and do righteous deeds, then God can be counted on to give you what you have earned, plus a bonus. Thus, the Quran promises,

Work and God will surely see your work. (9. 105)

Every soul shall be paid in full for what it has earned. (2. 282)

Those who believe and do deeds of righteousness and perform the prayer and pay the alms—their wage awaits them with the Lord. (2. 278)

According to the Qur'an God's love is thus reserved only for those who earn it. It says,

To those who believe and do righteousness, God will assign love. (19. 97).

So, the Qur'an assures us of God's love for the God-fearing and the good doers; but He has no love for sinners and unbelievers. Thus, in the Islamic conception, God is not all-loving. His love is partial and must be earned. The Muslim God only loves those who first love Him. His love thus rises no higher than the love which Jesus said even tax-collectors and unbeliever's exhibit.

Now don't you think this is an inadequate conception of God? What would you think of a parent who said to his children, "If you measure up to my standards and do as I say, then I will love you?" Some of you have had parents like that, who didn't love you unconditionally, and you know the emotional scars you bear as a result. As the greatest conceivable being, the most perfect being, the source of all goodness and love, God's love must be unconditional and impartial. Therefore, the Islamic conception of God seems to me to be morally deficient. I therefore cannot rationally accept it.

Undoubtedly, this difference between Jesus' Heavenly Father and the God of Mohammed is most clearly exhibited in the attitude we're commanded to have toward non-believers. Jesus said that we should love unbelievers, just as God does, even if they are our enemies. Mohammed's attitude and teaching were quite different. Early on in his career, when he himself was in the persecuted minority, Mohammed had a very positive attitude toward Jews and Christians, whom he called the "People of the Book" because of their adherence to the Bible. He believed that once the Jews understood his message, they would willingly convert to Islam. Passages in the Quran from this early period of Mohammed's life are quite positive toward Jews and Christians.

But when the Jews did not convert, but opposed Mohammed, he became increasingly embittered against them. As Mohammed acquired political and military strength, the persecuted prophet changed to the ruthless politician. He began to have the Jews in Medina, where his base of operations was, either killed or dispossessed. In the year 627, after an unsuccessful attack on Medina by the Arab army from Mecca, Mohammad rounded up hundreds of Jewish families in Medina. 700 Jewish men were put to the sword, and Mohammad had their wives and children sold into slavery.

Mohammad realized that in order to unify the fractious Arab tribes, outward expansion was necessary. So, he turned his eyes toward Syria and Iraq as obvious targets.

At this time, he lifted all protection from pagans. Unless they submitted to Islam, they were to be exterminated. The ninth chapter of the Quran comes from this period of Mohammad's life. It states that for four months pagan idolaters shall be left alone unmolested. Then comes this chilling command: "When the sacred months are past, kill the idolaters wherever you find them. Arrest them, besiege them, and lie in ambush everywhere for them. [But] If they repent and take to prayer and render the alms levy, allow them to go their way... they are your brothers in the Faith" (9.5, 11). Not only pagans, but even Jews and Christians, the once respected People of the Book, now also came under Mohammad's ban. Unless they submitted, they were likewise to be eliminated. Chapter 9 goes on to command Muslims: "Fight those from among the People of the Book who . . . do not embrace the true Faith until they pay tribute out of their own hand and are utterly subdued" (9.29). This chapter goes on to rebuke in the harshest terms any Muslim who refuses to go forth to fight: God will punish him and replace him with others (9.38-39). Muslims who refuse to fight will be smitten by God, either directly or — ominously—at the hands of faithful Muslims who do fight (9.52) "Wait if you will," the hesitant are told, "We too are waiting." But those who go forth in God's holy war are promised either victory or martyrdom (9.52). Those who die in God's cause are promised a Paradise of sensual delights: green gardens with flowing waters, silk couches, abundant wine, and voluptuous, dark-eyed virgins for their pleasure.

These are the last commands in the Qur'an with respect to unbelievers. Mohammad died shortly thereafter in 632 with plans before him for the attacks on neighboring nations. His successors carried out those attacks. In 633 the armies of Islam took Persia; in 635 Damascus fell; in 638 Jerusalem succumbed; in 640 Egypt was taken, and so on, right across North Africa to the Atlantic Coast.

We in the West with our democratic, liberal values tend to think that every religion surely shares our values. American officials have repeatedly said that we should not refer to the terrorists as "Islamic fundamentalists" because they are murderers, and no major religion advocate's murder. I wonder if these officials have ever read the ninth chapter of the Qur'an. The truth of the matter is Islam is a religion which enjoins violence and which, historically, has been propagated by violence.

Contrary to what you hear tirelessly repeated in the media, the word "Islam" does not mean "peace." That claim is simply linguistically false. "Islam" is the Arabic word for submission or surrender. That is what Muslims are called upon to do: to surrender everything to God. Thus, contrary to Western ways of thinking, Islam is not a church. It is crucial that we understand this. Islam is a total way of life: everything is to be submitted to God: the government, the economy, social mores, every aspect of society is submitted to God. Islam is thus all-consuming. The Western idea of separation of church and state is meaningless in Islam. For everything is to be submitted to God.

What this means is that it is really the so-called moderate Arab states like Egypt and Turkey, where you have a secular government distinct from Islamic law, in effect a separation of church and state, which are the ones who act inconsistently with Islam. They have adopted a Western model of governance, a separation of church and state, which is fundamentally incompatible with Islam. And that's why Islamic fundamentalists hate these moderate Arab regimes and want to overthrow them. The fundamentalists understand more accurately the true nature of Islam.

But of course, our public officials dare not say such a thing. We need the support of these moderate Arab states if our war against terrorism is to succeed. Therefore, moderate Muslims must be courted and reassured. And thus, we get all these politically correct, revisionist statements in the media that Islam means peace, that Muslims only fight in self-defense not aggression, that Islam condemns violence, and so forth. All of this is politically motivated revisionism which betrays the true character of Islam.

This is not to say that Islam sanctions all the atrocities perpetrated by groups like ISIL. I am not aware of anything in the Qur'an or in Sharia law that would sanction the rape of women or the execution of children in the name of Allah. The Prophet/Founder of Islam- Prophet Muhammed's teachings emphasized peace and forgiveness, but Islam has also historically included the use of violence in warfare. Islam has considered warfare to be a legitimate expression of religious faith. The Hadith includes saving of Muhammad that urge Muslims to practice Jihad. Nor am I saying that Muslims are violent people. I'm talking about theology, not people. We can be thankful that most Muslims are not fundamentalists, but are nominal Muslims, whose lives are far better than their theology. Indeed, they may know very little about Islamic theology. Asking a nominal Muslim what Islam teaches is rather like asking a nominal Catholic or Episcopalian what Christianity teaches!

So, I trust you can see how absurd the claim is that the God of Mohammed is the Father of Jesus Christ. The

Father of Jesus Christ loves sinners and commands us to love even our enemies, not to mention our neighbor. The God of Mohammad loves only those who love him, and he is an enemy to unbelievers. His followers are commanded to hunt down and kill unbelievers unless and until they submit. The God of the Qur'an is a defamation of the Heavenly Father proclaimed and revealed by Jesus.

To wrap up, then, we've seen, first, that the Christian concept of God as a Trinity is rationally unobjectionable and, second, that the Muslim concept of God is, by contrast, rationally objectionable because the God of Islam is morally deficient and therefore not the greatest conceivable being. As one theologian has rightly exclaimed, "Thank God for God!"

CHAPTER 4
THE NAMES OF JESUS.

AT LEAST 100 ANOINTED
NAMES OF JESUS
JESUS NAMES REIGNS FOREVER.

After personally experiencing the authority and power of Jesus as He spoke peace to a raging sea, the disciples were left sitting in the stillness, wet from the rain and wondering:

"Who is this man?" they asked. "Even the winds and waves obey him!" –Matthew 8:27 (NLT)

Over and again the Bible answers this amazing question by giving us glimpses of the character of Jesus through the names and descriptions we find of Him.

Here is a list of 100 Names of Jesus we find in the pages of the Bible. You can find the verses and study the context of each name by accessing the Logos Online Bible.

- Advocate (1 John 2:1)

- Almighty (Rev. 1:8; Mt. 28:18)

- Alpha and Omega (Rev. 1:8; 22:13)

- Amen (Rev. 3:14)

- Apostle of our Profession (Heb. 3:1)

- Atoning Sacrifice for our Sins (1 John 2:2)

- Author of Life (Acts 3:15)

- Author and Perfecter of our Faith (Heb. 12:2)

- Author of Salvation (Heb. 2:10)

- Beginning and End (Rev. 22:13)

- Blessed and only Ruler (1 Tim. 6:15)

- Bread of God (John 6:33)

- Bread of Life (John 6:35; 6:48)

- Capstone (Acts 4:11; 1 Pet. 2:7)

- Chief Cornerstone (Eph. 2:20)

- Chief Shepherd (1 Pet. 5:4)

- Christ (1 John 2:22)

- Creator (John 1:3)

- Deliverer (Rom. 11:26)

- Eternal Life (1 John 1:2; 5:20)

- Everlasting Father (Isa. 9:6)

- Gate (John 10:9)

- Faithful and True (Rev. 19:11)

- Faithful Witness (Rev. 1:5)

- Faith and True Witness (Rev. 3:14)

- First and Last (Rev. 1:17; 2:8; 22:13)

- Firstborn From the Dead (Rev. 1:5)

- God (John 1:1; 20:28; Heb. 1:8; Rom. 9:5; 2 Pet. 1:1;1 John 5:20; etc.)

- Good Shepherd (John 10:11,14)

- Great Shepherd (Heb. 13:20)

- Great High Priest (Heb. 4:14)

- Head of the Church (Eph. 1:22; 4:15; 5:23)

- Heir of all things (Heb. 1:2)

- High Priest (Heb. 2:17)

- Holy and True (Rev. 3:7)

- Holy One (Acts 3:14)

- Hope (1 Tim. 1:1)

- Hope of Glory (Col. 1:27)

- Horn of Salvation (Luke 1:69)

- I Am (John 8:58)

- Image of God (2 Cor. 4:4)

- King Eternal (1 Tim. 1:17)

- King of Israel (John 1:49)

- King of the Jews (Mt. 27:11)

- King of kings (1 Tim 6:15; Rev. 19:16)

- King of the Ages (Rev. 15:3)

- Lamb (Rev. 13:8)

- Lamb of God (John 1:29)

- Lamb Without Blemish (1 Pet. 1:19)

- Last Adam (1 Cor. 15:45)

- Life (John 14:6; Col. 3:4)

- Light of the World (John 8:12)

- Lion of the Tribe of Judah (Rev. 5:5)

- Living One (Rev. 1:18)

- Living Stone (1 Pet. 2:4)

- Lord (2 Pet. 2:20)

- Lord of All (Acts 10:36)

- Lord of Glory (1 Cor. 2:8)

- Lord of lords (Rev. 19:16)

- LORD [YHWH] our Righteousness (Jer. 23:6)

- Man from Heaven (1 Cor. 15:48)

- Mediator of the New Covenant (Heb. 9:15)

- Mighty God (Isa. 9:6)

- Morning Star (Rev. 22:16)

- Offspring of David (Rev. 22:16)

- Only Begotten Son of God (John 1:18; 1 John 4:9)

- Our Great God and Savior (Titus 2:13)

- Our Holiness (1 Cor. 1:30)

- Our Husband (2 Cor. 11:2)

- Our Protection (2 Thess. 3:3)

- Our Redemption (1 Cor. 1:30)

- Our Righteousness (1 Cor. 1:30)

- Our Sacrificed Passover Lamb (1 Cor. 5:7)

- Power of God (1 Cor. 1:24)

- Precious Cornerstone (1 Pet. 2:6)

- Prince of Peace (Isa. 9:6)

- Prophet (Acts 3:22)

- Resurrection and Life (John 11:25)

- Righteous Branch (Jer. 23:5)

- Righteous One (Acts 7:52; 1 John 2:1)

- Rock (1 Cor. 10:4)

- Root of David (Rev. 5:5; 22:16)

- Ruler of God's Creation (Rev. 3:14)

- Ruler of the Kings of the Earth (Rev. 1:5)

- Savior (Eph. 5:23; Titus 1:4; 3:6; 2 Pet. 2:20)

- Son of David (Lk. 18:39)

- Son of God (John 1:49; Heb. 4:14)

- Son of Man (Mt. 8:20)

- Son of the Highest God (Lk. 1:32)

- Source of Eternal Salvation for all who obey him (Heb. 5:9)

- The One Mediator (1 Tim. 2:5)

- The Stone the builders rejected (Acts 4:11)

- True Bread (John 6:32)

- True Light (John 1:9)

- True Vine (John 15:1)

- Truth (John 1:14; 14:6)

- Way (John 14:6)

- Wisdom of God (1 Cor. 1:24)

- Wonderful Counselor (Isa. 9:6)

- Word (John 1:1)

- Word of God (Rev. 19:13)

I have personally experienced Jesus through many of the names found on this list, but three of my greatest treasures is to know Him as my Friend, Advocate and Helper. One of earliest songs as a young born-again Christian, was and it is still inspiring l;" I have Jesus Christ who never fails." I sing that song on my wedding day and one of my children, Gideon, takes delight by singing that song. Another song back then and even now is the one that says:' "In the Name of Jesus Christ, every knee shall bow, and every tongue shall confess that Jesus Is the Lord of Lords and the King of kings."

CHAPTER 5

THE KINGDOM OF HEAVEN.

CAN YOU AND I VISUALIZE WITH THE EYE OF GOD THE KINGDOM OF HEAVEN?

COME WITH ME:

Some Bible terminology can seem strange to our modern ears. We are so removed from the original time and place of its writing that understanding its meaning can require some work. I think this is true about the phrase "the kingdom of heaven."

The kingdom of heaven is a central theme running all the way through the Gospel of Matthew. In fact, the phrase "the kingdom of heaven" is used over thirty times in Matthew's Gospel. However, many Christians are confused about what it means.

Interestingly, Matthew is the only Gospel writer to adopt this terminology. The others opt to use the phrase "the kingdom of God" instead. So, what is "the kingdom of heaven?"

Many believe that Matthew uses "the kingdom of heaven" instead of "the kingdom of God" simply to avoid using the term "God." It is certainly true that there was a Jewish tendency to avoid writing the divine name in the first century. However, Matthew does invoke the term "God" on numerous occasions.

Moreover, Matthew uses the phrase "the kingdom of God" on four occasions (Matt. 12:28; 19:24; 21:31, 43). So, there must be more going on than merely using the phrase "the kingdom of heaven" to avoid the word "God." There must be another purpose for this phrase.

A more plausible explanation is that Matthew did not want his Jewish readership to misunderstand the nature of the kingdom. The Jews were anticipating a physical kingdom, not a spiritual kingdom. However, while standing before Pilate at His trial, Jesus said, "My kingdom is not of this world. If my kingdom were of this world, my servants would have been fighting, that I might not be delivered over to the Jews. But my kingdom is not from the world" (John 18:36).

The use of the word "heaven" would certainly help emphasize and reinforce the spiritual nature of the kingdom.

Proclaiming the Kingdom of Heaven

Both the introduction to John the Baptist and the initiation of Jesus' ministry are accompanied with the proclamation to "repent, for the kingdom of heaven is at hand" (Matt. 3:2; 4:17). Just a few verses later, Matthew writes, "And he went throughout all Galilee, teaching in their synagogues and proclaiming the gospel of the kingdom and healing every disease and every affliction among the people" (Matt. 4:23 cf. Matt. 9:35). Using the phrase "the gospel of the kingdom," Matthew explicitly connects the kingdom of heaven with the gospel.

When Jesus sends out His disciples, He also commissions them to proclaim, "The kingdom of heaven is at hand" (Matt. 10:7). It is significant that John the Baptist, Jesus, and the disciples all preach the same message, and each follows with the command to repent. In fact, the call to repentance is grounded in the imminent coming of the kingdom of heaven. Everyone must repent because the kingdom of heaven is near.

Furthermore, those who disobey this command are like chaff that will be separated from the wheat and burned with unquenchable fire (Matt. 3:12). Therefore, rejecting the kingdom of heaven has eternal consequences.

In addition, proclaiming a message that is counter to the kingdom of heaven is condemnable. In Jesus' seven woes to the scribes and Pharisees, He says,

But woe to you, scribes and Pharisees, hypocrites! For you shut the kingdom of heaven in people's faces. For you neither enter yourselves nor allow those who would enter to go in. Woe to you, scribes and Pharisees, hypocrites! For you travel across sea and land to make a single proselyte, and when he becomes a proselyte, you make him twice as much a child of hell as yourselves (Matt. 23:13–15).

This is a stern warning not to draw people away from the kingdom of heaven by presuming that one can enter the kingdom by his own righteousness. In fact, Jesus said, "Not everyone who says to me, 'Lord, Lord,' will enter the kingdom of heaven, but the one who does the will of my Father who is in heaven" (Matt. 7:21).

Describing the Kingdom of Heaven

In contrast to the condemnation given to false teachers, Jesus offers blessings to members of the kingdom. Jesus begins His Sermon on the Mount discourse by blessing the "poor in spirit—for theirs is the kingdom of heaven" (Matt. 5:3). At the end of the Beatitudes, Jesus also references the kingdom of heaven. This time He says, "Blessed are those who are persecuted for righteousness' sake, for theirs is the kingdom of heaven" (Matt. 5:10). In either case, the kingdom is offered to those who put God's kingdom before their own self-interest.

Jesus' description of the kingdom of heaven almost seems upside-down. Jesus instructs His disciples, saying, "Among those born of women there has arisen no one greater than John the Baptist. Yet the one who is least in the kingdom of heaven is greater than he" (Matt. 11:11–12). Here Jesus is contrasting the natural birth into the world with the spiritual birth into the kingdom of heaven.

Multiple times in the Gospel of Matthew Jesus tells His listeners that they must become like children in order to enter the kingdom of heaven. He says, "Truly, I say to you, unless you turn and become like children, you will never enter the kingdom of heaven. Whoever humbles himself like this child is the greatest in the kingdom of heaven" (Matt. 18:3–4). He also said, "Let the little children come to me and do not hinder them, for to such belongs the kingdom of heaven" (Matt. 19:14–15). In the same way little children rely on the help and direction of their parents, citizens of the kingdom must rely on their Heavenly Father for everything. Jesus is commanding childlike trust in God to enter the kingdom.

After describing the importance of trusting and relying on God, Jesus gives His famous teaching on the difficulty of the rich person entering the kingdom of heaven. This is not a coincidence. The reader of Matthew's Gospel is meant to contrast the child, from the previous text, with the rich person. Unlike a child, who is dependent on others, the rich person can fall into the delusion of self-sufficiency. There is only room for one King in the kingdom of heaven, and that position is already taken.

Many of Jesus' parables focus explicitly on the kingdom of heaven. More specifically, there are a series of references to the kingdom of heaven in Matthew 13 and again in chapters 20 and 22. Each of these gives a glimpse of what the kingdom is like.

In describing the kingdom of heaven, Jesus draws comparisons to everyday experiences. He compares the kingdom to sowing seed in a field, which produces weeds with the wheat. The weeds are allowed to grow up with the wheat until the harvest; however, they will ultimately be bound into bundles and burnt (Matt. 13:24–30).

Similarly, the parable of the dragnet compares the kingdom of heaven to a net containing good and bad fish. They are all gathered but will later be separated. Jesus explains, "So it will be at the end of the age. The angels will come out and separate the evil from the righteous and throw them into the fiery furnace. In that place there will be weeping and gnashing of teeth" (Matt. 13:49–50). Even though God allows believers and unbelievers to live in His world together, they will be separated at the final judgment.

The kingdom of heaven is described as a valuable hidden treasure, which is worth more than all that one owns (Matt. 13:44) and something that should be sought after like a merchant in search of a pearl of great price (Matt. 13:45–46). The listener is meant to see how something that appears insignificant and small is of greatest value.

In the parable of the laborers in the vineyard, Jesus makes it clear the no one enters the kingdom based on their accomplishments. Instead, Jesus looks at the heart's response to His grace. From a human perspective, this seems counterintuitive. However, this parable displays the generosity of God as He gives out more grace than anyone deserves. In fact, the kingdom of heaven is precisely for those who do not deserve it but choose to put their faith in God (Matt. 21:31–32).

Timing the Kingdom of Heaven

The kingdom of heaven is spoken of in both present and future tense. The phrase is repeated that the kingdom of heaven is at hand (Matt. 4:17). Jesus' first coming is the inauguration of the kingdom. This means that Jesus is the immediate, present experience of the kingdom of heaven. For those who submit to Jesus, He will rule over their lives.

The kingdom of heaven is also spoken of in the future tense. One of the most notable instances of this takes place when Jesus is instructing his disciples on how to pray. Jesus prays, "Your kingdom come, your will be done, on earth as it is in heaven" (Matt. 6:10). This prayer only makes sense if the kingdom has not yet fully come.

Therefore, the kingdom of heaven is both now and not yet. It is present and it is future. It will finally culminate with the second coming of Jesus Christ. Jesus says,

When the Son of Man comes in his glory, and all the angels with him, then he will sit on his glorious throne.... Then the King will say to those on his right, "Come, you who are blessed by my Father, inherit the kingdom prepared for you from the foundation of the world." (Matt. 25:31, 34)

Applying the Kingdom of Heaven

The kingdom of heaven has important applications for us today. First, the message of the kingdom of heaven is a genuine offer from God to rule in the hearts of those who believe in His name. Submission to the kingship of God is what brings true freedom. Those who resist and reject God's kingdom are in bondage. This may sound counterintuitive, but those outside the kingdom of God are inside the kingdom of Satan (Eph. 2:1–3).

Second, as citizens of the kingdom of heaven, believers should be motivated to build the kingdom through proclaiming the kingdom. This was the central message of Jesus and the disciples, and it should be our message too.

Third, the kingdom of heaven provides comfort and hope for Christians who are suffering. God is King over all circumstances. No matter what happens in this life, all will be made right when God's kingdom comes

CHAPTER 6

APPLYING THE LORD'S SUPPER.

WHAT IS THE KINGDOM OF GOD LIKE?
(LUKE 13: 18-21)

UNDERSTANDING THE LORD'S DAY WITH THE EUCHARIST/HOLYCOMMUNION/LORD'S SUPPER.

Let us as part of the Body of CHRIST present ourselves as a living sacrifice. 'I beseech you brethren, by the mercies of God, that ye present your bodies a living sacrifices, holy, acceptable unto God which is your reasonable service." Romans 12; 1. Let us go, 'I was glad when they said unto me, let us go into the house of the Lord." (Psalms122;1)

If you have your Bibles, I'd invite you to turn with me to Luke, chapter 13 as we continue our way through the gospel together. In this passage Jesus tells two parables, two short stories describing what the kingdom of God is like.

We should be aware of a few things. First, 'Kingdom of God' is a favorite theme in Luke's gospel. This theme is found in all the gospels. Different terms are used. 'Kingdom of Heaven', typically Matthew will use that. That's a Hebrew idiom where you don't throw around the word God lightly so sometimes you substitute terms for God though you're referring to God, so 'Kingdom of

Heaven' instead of 'Kingdom of God' referring to the same idea though. 'Kingdom of Christ' is sometimes used, but it's all the same theme. The Kingdom of God refers to the reign of God in this world and especially in the hearts of men and women and boys and girls. It is a dynamic concept. It's not like a kingdom with walls around it. It's sort of a pulling up the drawbridge and filling up the moats with alligators and hunkering in. It's a kingdom that's dynamically going forth in this world and Jesus talks about it all the time. He is an agent of the kingdom. His gospel is bringing in the kingdom. The kingdom creates the church.

Those two things are related. In fact, they're inseparable, but they're distinguishable–the kingdom creates the people of the kingdom, the church of our Lord Jesus Christ, and for some reason Jesus thinks important here to pause and instruct his disciples in the nature of the kingdom and so you and I ought to be scratching our heads and wondering why. This is not the only time that Jesus does this, but here Luke, if you'll notice, connects these two parables with a 'therefore' in verse 18.

Now, what does that 'therefore' point back to? The immediate context is Jesus having done this amazing miracle for this woman who has been under a tremendous burden and satanic oppression for 18 years and the response of the religious leaders of his day who are present with him, is utter contempt for him and for her. And it seems that Jesus is saying to the disciples, "Don't be discouraged by their response to me. Don't think that just because the religious leaders of the day can see me do something like this and not only not get it and not only not believe my message, and not only not understand who I am, but oppose me, don't be discouraged by that.

The immediate assessment of your contemporaries is not an adequate indicator of the effectiveness of God's kingdom or its one day extent."

Now, that's a message that's important for us, too, because we live in a world, we live in a country which is increasingly hostile to the claims of the gospel. We have many contemporaries who think that they understand Christianity and they think that they've tried Christianity or tried the gospel or tried Jesus and they have weighed them in the balance and found them wanting and they have moved on and they're a little bit perturbed that you're still out there making claims for Jesus Christ.

And in that context, you can be tempted to do something and that is you can be tempted to change the message to make the message more palatable and attractive to the world and culture around you or you can be tempted to adopt different methods which end up changing the message that you are proclaiming. And so, Jesus words to his disciples of encouragement in the wake of his rejection by the religious leaders of his day about the kingdom are just as relevant to us today.

So, let's pray before we read God's Word.

Heavenly Father, this is Your Word and we ask that You would teach us about the kingdom, but also that we would so experientially be acquainted with the way of Your rule in our lives; that we understand that Your kingdom will not fail and that Your Word will not return void and that Your gospel when proclaimed will bring men and women and boys and girls to faith in Jesus Christ and that Your church will be built. Fix these as firm realities in our hearts so that we can continue to be faithful, joyful, energetic believing witnesses to Your kingdom and to Your gospel and to Your Son.

We ask this in Jesus' name. Amen.

Hear the Word of God beginning in Luke 13: 18:

"He said therefore, "What is the kingdom of God like? And to what shall I compare it? It is like a grain of mustard seed that a man took and sowed in his garden, and it grew and became a tree, and the birds of the air made nests in its branches."

And again, he said, "To what shall I compare the kingdom of God? It is like leaven that a woman took and hid in three measures of flour, until it was all leavened."

Amen. And thus, this reading of God's holy, inspired, and inerrant Word. May He write its eternal truth upon all our hearts.

Jesus in these two stories shows how something that looks small can become great. Something that looks insignificant but is in fact very significant; something that looks almost insubstantial can permeate everything. And He's telling these stories to encourage His disciples because He is perfectly aware of what the response to His ministry is and what the response to their ministries will be.

They are being called to preach Christ and his gospel in a world and into a culture that will overwhelmingly reject those realities. And if they view the kingdom by the measure of their contemporaries' acceptance or rejection of Christ, by their contemporaries' acceptance or rejection of their message, they will be discouraged because though they will see amazing things just like in Jesus' ministry, we saw amazing things. We saw amazing crowds follow Jesus' ministry from time to time and we saw amazing responses of faith to Jesus' ministry from time to time, and though the disciples, there will be days like the day of Pentecost when thousands come to trust in Christ, but there will be an overwhelming either yawn or rejection of their ministry, of their message, and of their mission by their contemporaries.

I mean, think of it, my friends. When Jesus first spoke these words there were no people in this world who called themselves Christian. Today there are about two billion people on this planet that call themselves Christians. So, Jesus is then proven in His story that the kingdom of God is going forth and though it is small as a mustard seed now it will grow to be a great tree in which the birds of the air will nest, but the disciples would not live and minister and see that big picture. And the fact of the matter is, none of us do and will. And so how we respond to the indifference or rejection of the kingdom and of the message of the kingdom and of the gospel and of the Lord Jesus Christ is very, very important to Jesus. And so, Jesus is wanting to encourage the disciples and He's wanting to encourage you and me.

And there's a very important message to us in our own day and time that I want us to take in both congregationally and personally. And here's the message: "Do not despise the day of small things. Do not judge God's kingdom by its immediate reception and effect either in our own hearts or the hearts of those that we long to see changed by the kingdom or by our communities' indifference or rejection of the message we proclaim.

You know, just over two centuries ago a German theologian looked out at his culture, and he saw the intellectual elite, the people in the universities, the people in the professional classes rejecting Christianity because the found it frankly unbelievable.

They were during the German enlightenment, and they were gripped by the new thinking that was spreading across Europe, and they were rejecting the message of Christianity, and he looked at that culture and he said, "You know, the kingdom is going to fail. The church is going to dwindle unless we come up with a message that this generation will believe." And so, he attempted to adapt the gospel message in order to make it more attractive and palatable to his contemporaries. His name was Friedrich Schleiermacher, and he gave a series of lectures or speeches, or addresses called On Christianity to Its Culture Despisers. Now his goal was not to destroy Christianity and empty the churches, but that is the effect of his work. He was the father of what we call today theological liberalism and wherever that belief reigns, the churches died.

But it was designed to make the kingdom grow and to make the church prosper and to make the gospel attractive and palatable and the idea was, we've got to change the message if the kingdom is going to grow, if the church is going to survive, if the message is going to prevail, we've got to change the message.

Now, evangelical Christians since that time have by and large rejected that approach. We know that God has given us the message in His Word, but we have tended to fall prey to a different kind of accommodation. And the kind of accommodation that we have been tempted to has been, one, to look around at the culture and then to look at the church and say, "You know, we're going to have to change the way we do church if we're going to be palatable and attractive to the culture."

When I was in seminary, and it feels like the Dark Ages

now, but it was only just over 25 years ago, the big thing was this. Some very, very intelligent people had looked across the landscape of the churches in America and they said, "You know, people respond to Christianity in America in the Protestant mainline churches basically with these two reactions. Church," they say, "is boring and irrelevant." And so, if we're going to reach this culture, we've got to make the church exciting and relevant. And so, the strategy was–create a church that is positioned to attract the unchurched by giving them something that is immediately and obviously relevant to them and exciting and attractive to them.

Now one of the consequences of that was that Bible preaching, for instance, was not one of the top five things that unchurched people found exciting and relevant about the church. And so, what happened in many, many churches is the preaching of the Bible disappeared.

And it's been fascinating. You know, in the last five years, survey after survey after survey has said that evangelical Christians, people who say they believe in the Bible and they're in church many, many Sundays out of the year, evangelical Christians don't know their Bibles. And my response whenever I read one of those surveys is, "Duh!" Because for the last three decades church has been managed by those who say, "Don't preach the Bible. That's boring and irrelevant. Give them something that they want. Give them excitement. Give them something that seems immediately relevant to them. Don't preach the Bible. That's boring!" And then we're surprised that people don't know their Bibles.

I like you went through periods of my life, especially in the teen years, when I found church deadly boring. And then one day I woke up and suddenly the faithful Bible ministry of my pastor and my elders didn't seem boring and irrelevant anymore. It was precisely what my soul needed and I'm so thankful that my pastor and elders didn't stop giving the means of grace as Jesus appointed so that when I woke up there was something still there for me to hear. There was still a saving truth to respond to. There was the substance of Jesus' message still there to arrest me. And I think it's important for us to remember that today.

Sometimes the things that we do may feel to you weak and ineffective. You know, it may seem that the means of grace and the message of the kingdom are small and weak and ineffective. And it may seem that the immediate results that the kingdom is having are insignificant, but Jesus says that God's kingdom is great, and its growth will be steady and continuous even it is not perceptible in the reactions of our immediate contemporaries to the message.

And that's very important for us to know. You know, we hear drastic reports, for instance, in America today about how many children of believing homes go off to college and in their early years of their career and never ever come back to a steady life of participation in the local congregation. And you have all these drastic reactions to these terrifying numbers and statistics that you hear.

And very often the reaction is, "We've got to do something completely different than we've ever done before."

And we forget that parents living the gospel before their children; teaching the gospel to their children; praying for their children; and bringing them to be with the people of God every Lord's Day has for two millennium nurtured Christianity. It looks weak. It looks small. It looks insignificant, but God has appointed His means of grace to work in the kingdom He's built.

Or we look at the church and we say, "The church is up against it. The church is struggling. She's weak within and wracked with all the same kinds of social challenges and problems that the culture is wracked with around us and the message seems so weak and contemptible. It seems so unpalatable, and it seems so unpopular."

But when the Word is preached and baptism and the Lord's Supper is administered and prayer is offered as the people of God gather, God blesses His means of grace. The kingdom goes forth. It creates the church, God's means of grace work in the world. And Jesus is encouraging us here to believe that God is building His church. I mean, that, in the end is the point, isn't it, that you can study all that the New Testament says about the kingdom of God and in none of it will you get this message: "The building of God's kingdom is up to you." Now, we get to participate in it, and we must respond to it, but God's kingdom is God's kingdom, and He builds His kingdom and what He builds cannot fail and the way that He builds His kingdom will not fail. It is our job to believe that and to respond to that and to live accordingly with that–with that hope that His message will prevail in this world and that the kingdoms of this world will become the kingdom of our Lord and of His Christ and He will reign forever and ever.

It's so important that we believe that. It's so important that we understand that, or we'll be tempted to change the message, or we'll be tempted to denigrate the means that He has given for the building up of His church or the message that has been given for the kingdom to announce.

Maybe you've been praying in vain for God's kingdom to manifest itself in the heart of a friend or a child or a brother or a sister or a parent.

Do not despise the day of small things because there are things that look insignificant to our eyes and the Lord is doing something deeper and bigger than we could ever imagine.

Do not despise these small beginnings, for the LORD rejoices to see the work begin, to see the plumb line in Zerubbabel's hand. (The seven lamps represent the eyes of the LORD that search all around the world.)

Zechariah 4:10

Jesus wants His disciples to be encouraged by that even when the religious leaders of His day are rejecting Him. Even after He's done a mighty miracle, they can reject Him. And Jesus says, "The kingdom in the end will not be judged by them, but when God unveils that kingdom, when He shows to all of us what He's been doing, our breath will be taken away." And we'll say, "Jesus, what you said was true. It may be like those tiny little mustard seeds, but it's a huge tree now. It may be like that leaven, but you can't even detect but that leaven has spread through everything now and leavened the whole. Your kingdom has grown."

I love what J. C. Ryle says.

"Christianity is a religion which at first seems so feeble and helpless and powerless that it could not live. Its first founder was one who was poor in this world, and He ended His life by dying the death of a malefactor on the cross. Its first adherence was a little company whose number probably did not exceed a thousand when the Lord Jesus left this world. Its first preachers were a few fishermen and publicans who were most of them unlearned and ignorant men. Its first starting point was a despised corner of the earth called Judea, a petty tributary province of the vast empire of Rome. Its first doctrine was eminently calculated to call forth the enmity of the natural heart, Christ crucified was to the Jews a stumbling block and to the Greeks, foolishness. Its first movements brought down its friends' persecution from all quarters. Pharisees and Sadducees and Jews and Gentiles, ignorant idolaters and self-conceited philosophers all agreed in hating and opposing Christianity. It was a sect everywhere spoken against. There are no empty assertions. They're simple historical facts which no one can deny. If ever there was a religion that was a little grain of seed at its beginning, that religion was the gospel, but the progress of the gospel is great and steady and continuous."

It is true, my friends. Do not think that you have to position and maneuver yourself for God to work even in this hard-hearted world because the kingdom will be built. The only question is will we have the pleasure of participating in that. If we trust Him to build His kingdom and if we use His means, we will have the joy of participating in that, but we'll get none of the credit for ourselves because He's building His kingdom.

Our Heavenly Father, we thank You for the kingdom which is not of this world which You are building in the reign that You have established in our hearts by the gospel and the church that You have created because of the work of that kingdom. And we pray, O Lord, in a day in time when the world says to us, "Your message is no longer compelling to us. Your mission is despicable to us. Your claims are uncompelling to us.

We pray, O Lord, that we will hear the words of Jesus speaking more loudly over those messages of rejection and saying the kingdom of God is like a mustard seed, my child. And then we pray that you would give us faith even of the size of the mustard seed for we know that if we but trust Your ends and Your means we will by grace be able to move mountains.

We ask these prayers in Jesus' name. Amen.

The Apostle Paul tells us of the origin of the Lords' Supper and its institution in 1 Corinthians 11.

He puts it this way:

"For I received from the Lord that which I delivered to you, that the Lord Jesus in the night in which he was betrayed took bread, and when he had given thanks, he broke it, and said, "This is my body which is for you. Do this in remembrance of me." In the same way he took the cup also, after supper, saying, "This cup is the new covenant in my blood. Do this, as often as you drink it, in remembrance of me. For as often as you eat this bread and drink the cup, you proclaim the Lord's death until he comes.

Therefore, whoever eats the bread or drinks the cup of the Lord in an unworthy manner shall be guilty of the body and the blood of the Lord. But a man must examine himself, and in so doing, he is to eat of the bread and drink of the cup. For he who eats and drinks, eats and drinks judgment to himself if he does not judge the body rightly."

Amen. And thus ends this reading of God's holy Word.

The Lord's Supper is a sacrament. It's a sign and seal of God's covenant of grace. It's something that God gives us to confirm His promise to us and to strengthen our faith in that promise, to assure us of His love and of His saving purposes for us. It's a God-appointed means to grow us in grace. It's one of the principled ways that God has appointed or ordained to strengthen us in the Christian life.

And the Lord's Supper we feed on Christ by faith and are strengthened by him. So, the Lord's table is for those who are believing, who are trusting in the Lord Jesus Christ and so I would invite to this table, the Lord's table, all of you who trust in Jesus Christ alone for your salvation as He is offered in the gospel and who have joined yourselves to the body of Christ, the church.

If you are here with us today and you are not a believer, you are welcome, but I charge you not to come to this table because, if you do, not believing, you will be precisely the one about whom Paul is speaking about not judging the body rightly. Do not eat and drink condemnation to yourself. Instead, I would charge you to wait and think and pray. Think of your heart and your sin. Think of the claims of Christ the Savior, think of the gospel of grace in the scripture, and then repent and believe and then the next time we gather at the Lord's table, come as a brother or a sister in Christ with us, trusting in Him, and we receive you gladly in the Lord.

Let us set apart these common elements to a holy use by prayer. Let's pray.

Eternal God, you are the Lord of creation and of redemption. Triune God, Father, Son, and Holy Spirit, you have made yourself manifest in the incarnation of our Lord Jesus Christ. We gather at the Lord's table today at Your own bidding and we acknowledge Your grace to us. Make these common elements to serve as Your means of grace to Your people and grant that we would receive them by faith and so taste of heavenly mercies that are bestowed only by the Holy Spirit. Lift our hearts to heaven on high that we might feed on the risen and ascended Christ in His glorious humanity by faith. We ask this all through Jesus Christ our Lord. Amen.

Since the Lord's Supper is for professing believers in Jesus Christ who have discerned the body of the Lord, it's appropriate that we confess our faith together before we come to this table. Let us do this using the Apostles' Biblical Creed.

Christian, what do you believe?

I believe in God the Father, Almighty,

Maker of Heaven and Earth:

And in Jesus Christ, his only Son, our Lord.

Who was conceived by the Holy Ghost,

born of the Virgin Mary, suffered under Pontius Pilate,

was crucified, dead, and buried. he descended into hell.

the third day he arose again from the dead.

he ascended into heaven,

 and sat on the right hand of God the Father Almighty.

from thence he shall come to judge

the quick and the dead.

I believe in the Holy Ghost.

the holy catholic church.

the communion of saints.

the forgiveness of sins.

the resurrection of the body.

and life is everlasting. Amen.

Jesus Christ reaffirms the Ten Commandments. Since Jesus Christ was clear that He obeyed His Father's commandments, then in order to truly follow Him, we must obey the Father's commandments as well. They remind us of our sins for we have broken each of these commandments. They remind us of the perfection of Christ's life and sacrifice because he obeyed these commandments perfectly and died under their penalty in our place. And He did so not only that we would be forgiven, but so that we would be changed and enabled to walk with God in His will. And so, these commandments also remind us what the godly life of a walk with Christ looks like. So let us repeat these Ten Commandments as we prepare to come to the Lord's table.

1. You shall have no other gods before Me.

2. You shall not make for yourself an idol. You shall not worship them or serve them.

3. You shall not take the name of the Lord your God in vain.

4. Remember the Sabbath day, to keep it holy.

5. Honor your father and your mother.

6. You shall not murder.

7. You shall not commit adultery.

8. You shall not steal.

9. You shall not bear false witness against your neighbor.

10. You shall not covet.

However, JESUS CHRIST summarized all of God's laws in two great commandments, "You shall love the love the LORD your God with your heart, with all your soul, and with all your mind, "This is the first and great commandment. And the second is like the first: "You shall love your neighbor as yourself." Jesus Christ said," On these two commandments hang all the law and the Prophets" Matthew 22:40

REFLECTIVE PRAYER ON THE JOURNEY.

Let us pray.

Lord, it cost death and shed blood and humiliation, and shame of the Lord Jesus to forgive us our sins, to make us presentable to You. There was no other good enough to pay the price of sin. He only could unlock the gates of heaven and let us in. He who thought it not robbery to be equal with God but made himself nothing. But the foxes have holes and the birds of the air have their nests, but the

Son of Man has nowhere where to lay His head.

We thank You for Gethsemane. We thank You for Calvary. We thank You, O Lord, for a substitute, one who bore our sin and our shame in His body upon the tree.

We thank You this morning afresh for the gospel, for grace that pardons all sin, that by faith alone in Jesus Christ alone we may stand before You as adopted children and heirs, joint heirs with Jesus Christ.

Help us, O Lord, as we go our various ways just now to rejoice and treasure the gospel and treasure Christ. That's where our hearts would be today–in love with Jesus.

Oh, that we might love You more than we do. Have everything that there is of us. Take us and use us and do with us as You will because whatever You do it will be for our good. And we ask it in Jesus' name. Amen.

CHAPTER 7
IS IT UPSIDE DOWN?

IS THE KINGDOM OF GOD UPSIDE DOWN?
WHY NOT?
UPSIDE DOWN AND DOWNWARD UP
APPROACH TO THE KINGDOM OF GOD.

As parents to four children, three boys and a girl, we had challenges raising our children through different stages of their lives from conception until they each became young adults. There were parenting seasons I referred to as tsunami passages. Tanami is a Japanese word with a double root: tsu; meaning port of harbor, and Nami, meaning wave. The word looks innocuous in simple transition, but to those who live on the rim of the Pacific it can spell disaster. Extremely tough seasons with uncertainties. The challenge taught me to look inward before looking outside. How can I live as a father if/when I am not living as an example? One of the children called my attention to my struggles when he said," Dad, why are you worried when you preached and told us not to be worried?" Then, my daughter stepped into my car early morning as we were heading for her school in Azusa, California with stuff in addition to her school backpack. Surprisingly, I asked her, "Esty, the best, what is this? "She quickly responded, "Dad, I am taking this stuff to my classmate because I saw that she needed these things.

I just want to share."

Don't get me wrong, my children were amazing, and of course, young children growing up are indeed innocent of much of the evil of this world. Innocent will say. Really! Not exactly? Why? "In sin my mother conceived me." (Psalms 51:5) When I was little, I used to fight my sister Martina despite her kindness to me. My Godly precious mother now in heaven will often pull me aside to remind me, "do you know that your small sister cares about you. Please stop fighting her. Mother and my sister were right, but I was wrong."

But what struck me quickly as a dad was how selfish we inherently are, from the moment we show up.

It was new and hard-hitting for me to realize we must teach our kids how to share, how to be respectful, how to get along, how to not hit others. Our natural tendencies aren't great. In our fallenness, we are all about ourselves, and we need to intentionally be taught to love God and others.

But when Jesus arrived on earth, He made a bold pronouncement:

"The Kingdom of Heaven has come near." (Matthew 3:2)

Really? Isn't Heaven "up there" somewhere, beyond this earth?

Yes, there is another realm out there, but when Jesus showed up, something changed.

Starting with Him, the Kingdom of Heaven had invaded earth. No longer the ethereal "other" place, God's Kingdom was actively taking over the planet. Jesus was setting up a new realm on earth, where He would rule, and which would spread worldwide (Matthew 13:31-33).

This new Kingdom obviously has a King, and, like all kingdoms, has rules for living. The rules are God's perfect rule, the exact way that He wants us to live, and are modelled for us completely in the example and teachings of Christ. Through Jesus, we learn how this Kingdom works and how Christians live as its citizens.

Since humanity is sinful, this godly Kingdom challenges our natural selfishness and preferred ways of living.

In fact, this Kingdom often seems completely backwards and upside-down to how our flesh and this world tell us to live.

And yet, to be men of God, to be men of the Kingdom, we must deny ourselves, take up our cross, and follow in the footsteps of Jesus in the way He lived and calls us to live (Matthew 16:24-25; 1 John 2:6).

As men, we need to learn, live, and share the ways of this Kingdom.

So, what does that look like?

In the upside-down Kingdom:

God is God

Ever since Eden, humans wanted to take control and be their own god (Genesis 3:1-6). We wanted to live our own ways, following Adam and Eve's example (Isaiah 53:6). But in this Kingdom, there is no sharing of rule: God is God, and we are not. Citizens bow their knees to Him and acknowledge the one Lord over all (1 Corinthians 8:6).

Lower is Higher. The Way Up is the Way Down!

"Climb the ladder!" It's the cry of Western culture. More prestige, more followers, more clicks and likes, more power, more money. We greatly admire those who climb their way to the top. But Jesus was at the top, and left it all to make Himself nothing, living a lowly, poor, and humble life, dying on the Cross (Philippians 2:5-8). And He explicitly told us that the only way to get "higher" in this Kingdom was to lower yourself, like He did, choosing the humblest pathways and places (Matthew 23:11-12; Luke 14:9-11). We become greater in the Kingdom by becoming less, not climbing higher.

Others are First

As mentioned, from infancy on, we are all about ourselves. We need to be taught to think of others, and it's a life-long lesson. Jesus lived a life that put others before Himself, and we too are called to lay down ourselves for the sake of others (Philippians 2:3-4; 1 John 3:16). With a natural tendency towards selfishness and a culture that screams "Me!" men prove ourselves part of this Kingdom when we put others first, as Jesus did.

Weak is Strong

The world values strength, and so do men, but our King specifically chose worldly weakness— when He walked the earth—no armies, no money, no political power, no coercion. He laid down His life in weakness, allowing His body to be broken on the Cross, so that God's strength could be displayed through the resurrection (2 Corinthians

13:4). The apostle Paul noted that his preaching skills were thoroughly unimpressive, but still contained God's power (1 Corinthians 2:1-5). He noted that in his moments of weakness, God's strength met him there (2 Corinthians 12:9). Kingdom strength looks different than worldly strength because it is in the absence of our strength that God shows off His strength most spectacularly. Men of the Kingdom embrace this dynamic.

Enemies are Loved

When my kids were little, they hit each other quite a lot. The idea of, "You hurt me, I hurt you back," is instinctive to us, and reinforced in our culture as well as globally by the kingdoms of this world. But in Christ, God shows great kindness to His enemies (Romans 5:10). He loves His enemies, and Jesus said that when we love our enemies, we look like our Father in Heaven (Matthew 5:43-48). In this Kingdom, men lay aside our natural desire to harm enemies, and instead embrace them with love, as God did with us.

Inside is Out

Common sense says that if you want to change something about yourself, you change the behavior. Men like this approach a lot. But in the upside-down Kingdom, we can't change ourselves—we need to be changed by God (2 Corinthians 3:18). The Holy Spirit does the work of transforming our hearts and minds (Ezekiel 11:19-20; Romans 12:2), and as this changes inwardly, outer behavior follows.

A man's greatest effort goes into connecting with God,

so that He might transform us inside, that godly behavior would flow outwards from that.

Grace is Enough

Finally, unlike worldly nations, a man can't earn his way into citizenship in this Kingdom. You can only enter it by receiving it as a gift from the King (Ephesians 2:8-9; Titus 3:4-7). Grace is the ticket of entry, and when our flesh and our culture push men to achieve and earn, grace stands against those attitudes and issues a simple invitation: trust the King, and enter the Kingdom prepared for you (Matthew 25:34). One of the earliest definitions of Grace that ministered and helped my walk in Christ is that GRACE is; God Riches At Christ Expense.

CHAPTER 8
CALL INTO CONFLICTS.

JESUS CHRIST CALLED HIS FOLLOWERS TO CONNECT.

JESUS CHRIST CALLED HIS EMERGING LEADERS.

The second phase in Jesus' disciple-making process invited disciples to connect with other believers. After John the Baptist was arrested by Herod Antipas, Jesus stepped up and started preaching His message of repentance and faith (Matthew 4.12-17 ESV). He also worked to gather a small group of emerging leaders who could carry that message forward.

The first two emerging leaders that Jesus enlisted were Peter and Andrew. He said, "Follow me, and I will make you fishers of men" Matthew 4.19 ESV. Next, He invited James and John to join the group and follow Him Matthew 4.21 ESV. When they agreed to follow Jesus, they were making a commitment to Him, but they were also making a commitment to each other.

The group lived in community. They went with Jesus as He traveled, preached, and healed. They watched and learned from Him as He cast out demons, announced the coming of God's Kingdom, and challenged the hypocrisy of the religious leaders who loved compliance with the law more than people.

A commitment to connect.

To grow spiritually, you must make a commitment to connect. Specifically, Jesus called His followers to make four important connections:

1. Disciples must connect with Jesus Christ. Jesus issued a clear call for people to follow Him. Spiritually curious people can't remain seekers forever. At some point, they must decide about whether to trust Jesus and follow Him or not. One cannot be a disciple of Jesus if he isn't a follower of Jesus.

2. Disciples must connect to a church through baptism. Following Jesus is a personal decision, but it involves public actions; it can't be done in secrecy (Luke 9.26 ESV). After a person has decided to follow Jesus, the next step is to go public with that decision by being baptized. While baptism doesn't save a person, it's the way Jesus gave us to announce that we're following Him and connect with a church family.

3. Disciples must connect with other believers in community. In addition to aligning themselves with Jesus in public, Jesus' followers also chose to do life together. They spent time together and shared meals. They learned to navigate the ups and downs of life together. Small groups provide the best environment for spiritual growth today because they allow you to know others and be known by them.

4. Disciples must connect with Jesus' cause. Slowly but surely, Jesus' disciples stopped watching Jesus do

everything and started joining in on what Jesus was doing. They got involved, serving others with their unique talents, gifts, and abilities. As you give and serve, you contribute to the cause of Christ in the world. The Great Commission that Jesus Christ laid out in the four synoptic gospels is never to be taken as "great suggestions" but are met to be mandatory for every believer.

CHAPTER 9
THE COST OF THE KINGDOM.

DO YOU KNOW THE COST FOR THE KINGDOM OF GOD?

Have you ever been to a restaurant and ordered something only to find that it was nothing like you imagined? For instance, when in Hawaii in 2021, with my wife, I ordered something that I thought would have been a hearty appetizer only to find out that it was not. I was sincerely wrong. A precious couple, The Williams, that we met with through The Omotoshos, of Messiah Baptist Church, Los Angeles, sponsored. us to the vacation. Similarly, in Mark 10:35–45 James and John approached Jesus to place an order for something they wanted Jesus to do for them when He became King, only to find out they really didn't understand what was on the menu.

James and John quietly approach Jesus and ask, when you come into your kingdom, "Grant us to sit, one at your right hand and one at your left." In other words, after Jesus does the heavy lifting, overthrows the powers that be, and rules in Jerusalem, they want to make sure they have a prominent position in His cabinet. Jesus immediately responds telling them they really don't know what they are asking, given the fact that Jesus was not going to seize power through violence and usher His kingdom in through force. Rather, Jesus would usher in His kingdom in a completely unconventional countercultural way.

In this exchange, Jesus clarifies for James and John, as

well as us, at least three things about the nature of His kingdom.

Jesus' kingdom is about the power of love rather than the love of power.

James and John wanted to rule with Jesus. Were they wrong in asking this? Absolutely not! Humans were created to rule. Adam and Eve were vice-regents (prince and princess) under the lordship of God. But the temptation to rule themselves overcame the rule of God. In other words, the love (or lust) of power corrupted and overcame the power of love.

Here Jesus teaches James and John that His kingdom is marked by the power of love rather than the love (or lust) for power.

We live in a culture that finds power intoxicating. Don't misunderstand power. Power comes in many shapes and sizes. Power can be manifested in freedom of individual expression, money, purchases (buying power), positions (businesses, organizations, or boards), images (seen through the clothes we wear, the cars we drive, the company we work for, the educational institution we attended, or how others perceive us), or achievements (like educational or vocational). These things, and more, allure and entice people to forego morals, take short cuts, and hurt others. They also create an insatiable desire for [selfishly obtaining] more. In short, these things awaken people's appetite, like Adam and Eve, to the love of power.

John would go on to write, "Do not love the world or the things in the world" (1 John 2:15). John would also describe the love of these things above as desires of the flesh, which are from the world.

However, Christ's kingdom overcomes the love of the

world, for it was brought forth by a love of God and love for the world.

Therefore, those who are part of His kingdom live by the power of love rather than a love for power. But what does this look like? The next two points explain.

Jesus' kingdom is about giving up one's life in order to give life.

In asking whether James and John could drink from His cup or be baptized with the same baptism, Jesus alludes to his sacrificial and substitutionary death on a cross.

Jesus inevitably shares with James and John that to be positioned with Him means one must take up their cross and follow in His footsteps.

Thus, the one who follows Jesus will give up their life for the sake of others. Kingdom living means we give up so that others may go up. We give our life so that others might live.

I think this aspect of following Jesus is the scariest, and especially for Americans doesn't quite allure and hook us in as fish swimming in the sea of self-seeking and self-aggrandizement. Yet the reality is when imputed with the heart of the kingdom, Christ followers don't look for what others can do for them—including God Himself—but what they can do for the glory of God and the good of others. They look for ways to inject themselves in the brokenness of the world and in individual lives to see how they can be used as an agent of redemption, of reconciliation.

Just as a seed dies to give birth to a plant or tree, we die to ourselves in order that life may emerge from the darkened soil of human depravity and brokenness.

Death to ourselves, giving up our lives, is marked by sacrifice, substitution, and suffering. Of course, we are not called to die for the sins of the world, but we are called to die to self and to live for God so that others might experience abundant life in Christ. I know, suffering is scary and far from fun. But keep in mind, that suffering only lasts for the night (this life), but joy comes in the morning (at the Second Coming of Christ when He consummates His kingdom).

Jesus' kingdom measures greatness (or success) not by how many are serving you, but how many you are serving.

James and John sought a promotion. They wanted to be raised to General 1 and 2, but at best, their request made them look like Tweedledee and Tweedledum.

Jesus' response communicates that success in His kingdom isn't built on rising to the top whereby you have much power and many people serving you but is about sinking to the bottom whereby you can serve others.

It's not that you forget (theoretically) your position or place; it's just you leave it, go down to the bottom, and take as many people back up with you to your position. Just as Jesus left His throne and made His way to a trough and then a cross in order to identify with us and take our sin upon Himself so that we may be restored image-bearers who rule and reign with Him forever; so, we too humbly enter the brokenness, hopelessness, pain, and suffering of others in an effort to share with and show them the redemptive kingdom of Christ.

Jesus' kingdom is counter-cultural to our understanding of success.

Jesus' kingdom inverts service from top to bottom. It's not about how many people we have serving under us, but how many people we are serving above.

Thus, Jesus' kingdom metric of success is not how clean we are in our nice cozy comforts of prominence and power, but how dirty we are in our uncomfortable unselfish positions of servitude and sacrifice.

In closing I know that we fail many times to realize that we are part of Christ's kingdom, given that there's very little talk in church circles about the kingdom. But the truth is, we are part of His kingdom and will one day rule and reign with Him forever. Thus, we must clarify the nature and characteristics of His Kingdom and His rule. If not, we may find ourselves thinking Jesus' kingdom is one thing when it is something entirely different.

James and John realized that Christ inaugurated His kingdom by the power of love, which was demonstrated by service, sacrifice, substitution, and suffering. To a large degree Jesus did all the heavy lifting in establishing His kingdom. However, He hasn't done all the heavy lifting so that we can request high-ranking positions in His kingdom—or live high-ranking self-centered prosperous lives. Rather His heavy lifting paves the way in which we follow Him to advance His kingdom on planet earth through love, service, sacrifice, substitution, and suffering. And it is through that kingdom life we manifest the nature of Christ's kingdom and one day experience the weight of the words from our King, "Well done, my good and faithful servant."

CHAPTER 10

PROBING QUESTIONS- WHAT HAPPENS IN THE BOOK OF ACTS?

PROBING QUESTIONS: What if Jesus Never Intended His Followers to Form a Church as we Know it Today?

I looked at where the Bible talks about the kingdom of God and where it talks about church. What I learned is shocking. Jesus teaches about the kingdom of God, not church.

These are New Testament Considerations

Both the church and the kingdom of God (along with the kingdom of Heaven) are New Testament concepts. None of these terms occur in the Old Testament. Since Jesus comes to fulfill the Law (Matthew 5:17), the kingdom of God must be one way he intends to do so.

Jesus Teaches about the Kingdom of God, not Church

Jesus talks much about the kingdom of God (Heaven) and little about the church: fifty-four times versus three. Clearly Jesus focuses his teaching on the kingdom of God. If the kingdom of God is so important to Jesus, it should be important to us as well.

A Change Occurs in Acts

A transition of emphasis happens in the book of Acts, with twenty-one mentions of church and only six mentions of the kingdom of God. Early on Jesus's followers shift their focus from the kingdom of God to the church.

This is logical because a church is a tangible result while the kingdom of God is a more ethereal concept. But just because this is a logical shift, that doesn't make it right.

Jesus's Followers Focus on Church

The rest of the New Testament (Romans through Revelation) emphasizes church over the kingdom of God: ninety times versus eight.

Even though the early followers of Jesus favor the practice of church over the concept of the kingdom of God, the fact remains that their practice of church then is far different from ours today.

Today's church should push aside her traditions and practices to replace them with what Jesus teaches about the kingdom of God. It will change everything.

(Here's the background:)

The word church occurs 114 times in the Bible, all in the New Testament. Of the four accounts of Jesus, church only occurs in Matthew and then just three times. Acts, the book about the early church, mentions church twenty-one times.

The word church occurs in most of the rest of the New Testament books (fifteen of them).

Instead of church, Jesus talks about the kingdom of

God. The phrase, kingdom of God, occurs sixty-eight times in the Bible, again, all in the New Testament.

Most occurrences are in the four biographies of Jesus, accounting for fifty-four of its sixty-eight appearances. Acts mentions the kingdom of God six times, with only eight occurrences popping up in the rest of the New Testament.

Matthew generally writes using the kingdom of Heaven instead of the kingdom of God. He uses kingdom of Heaven thirty-one times and is the only writer in the Bible to use this phrase.

By comparing parallel passages in Matthew, Mark, and Luke, we see the same account with the only difference being that Matthew writes kingdom of Heaven whereas Mark and Luke use kingdom of God.

Clearly Matthew, the only biblical writer to use the kingdom of Heaven, equates it to the kingdom of God. Additionally, Matthew uses the kingdom of God five times.

CHAPTER 11
DIFFERENT
GROUPS/CLIQUES/VERSIONS

ARE YOU CALLED TO PREACH AND LIVE FOR
CHRIST JESUS AND HIS KINGDOM? OR FOR
YOUR CHURCH, DENOMINATION,MINISTRIES
ORGANIZATIONS, ETC.?

WHAT THEN IS THE KINGDOM OF GOD?
COME WITH ME TO THE UNDERSTANDING
ITS MEANING/ESSENSE.

The Kingdom of God is mentioned throughout the Old and New Testaments of the Bible. In fact, the phrase "Kingdom of God" is used over 70 times in the New Testament - with the Gospel of Matthew over 30 times.

As a Christian, it's essential to understand the meaning behind this phrase, which is often confusing for many Christians and non-Christians. If someone asked you what the kingdom of God meant, would you know how to answer them?

"For the kingdom of God is not a matter of eating and drinking but of righteousness and peace and joy in the Holy Spirit." ~ Romans 14:17

Let's look at the original Greek and Hebrew meaning of the phrase, the different phrases used throughout the Bible, what it means to seek first the Kingdom of God, and how to live and pray with the Kingdom of God in mind.

Origin and Meaning of the Kingdom of God

From the coming of Jesus Christ to establish His Kingdom, through the whole story of redemptive history and the Church, we see a clear picture of the Gospel. According to Easton's Bible Dictionary, this "kingdom of God" is mentioned in the Scriptures in several different ways throughout the Old and New Testaments: Matthew 6:33, Mark 1:14-15, and Luke 4:43 all refer to the "kingdom of Christ."

Matthew 13:41 and 20:21 refer to the "kingdom of Christ and God."

Ephesians 5:5 refers to the "kingdom of David."

Mark 11:10 refers to "the kingdom."

Matthew 3:2, 4:17, 8:12, 13:14, and 13:29 refer to the "Kingdom of Heaven."

Even though the exact wording differs between Christ, God, and heaven, all Scriptures embody the same concept with different aspects.

The Kingdom of God also reflects the prophetic fulfillment of God's promises to Israel and the whole world. The Old Testament prophets, such as Isaiah and Daniel, foretold the coming of a messianic King who would establish God's reign of peace, justice, and righteousness on earth. This anticipation finds its fulfillment in Jesus Christ, who inaugurated the Kingdom through His life, death, and resurrection, and will consummate it at His second coming.

Here are three things that the Kingdom of God means:

1. The rule of Jesus Christ on earth and in heaven

2. The blessings and advantages that flow from living under Christ's rule

3. The subjects of this kingdom, or the Church

Just how important was the understanding of the Kingdom of God? John the Baptist used it often as he called for to repent, for the kingdom of God is near" (Matthew 3:2). Jesus Christ himself not only said, "the kingdom of God is nearby. Repent and believe" (Matthew 4:17), but he also used it when teaching his disciples how to pray "your kingdom come" (Matthew 6:10), in the Beatitudes "theirs is the kingdom of heaven" (Matthew 5:3 and 10). At the Last Supper, "I will not drink again of the fruit of the vine until that day when I drink it anew in the kingdom of God" (Mark 14:25).

Why Does Matthew Use 'Kingdom of Heaven' Instead of 'Kingdom of God'?

Throughout the Gospel of Matthew, we see Matthew using the phrase "kingdom of heaven" when referring to the announcement of the rule of Jesus Christ and the good news of His reign. He does this out of sensitivity to the Jews who avoid mentioning the sacred name of God. The doctrine is the same, and there is no different view or meaning of the kingdom of God versus heaven; Matthew is simply using an indirect phrase that respects the reader.

"Not everyone who says to me, 'Lord, Lord,' will enter the kingdom of heaven, but the one who does the will of my Father who is in heaven." ~ Matthew 7:21

"Blessed are the poor in spirit, for theirs is the kingdom of heaven." ~ Matthew 5:3

The term "Kingdom of Heaven" also emphasizes the heavenly origin and nature of this Kingdom, distinguishing it from earthly kingdoms. Matthew's choice of wording reflects a deep reverence for God's holiness, aligning with Jewish traditions that often-avoided direct references to God's name. This distinction underscores the transcendent and divine character of God's Kingdom, which contrasts with worldly powers and authorities.

What is the difference? There is no genuine distinction between the Kingdom of Heaven and the Kingdom of God. The two expressions are basically two unique approaches to show the same thing: a system of government or a kingdom that is ruled and controlled by God. The authority to rule was given to Jesus Christ by the Father, who is now situated at the right hand of the Father. At an assigned future time, at the hour of Christ's subsequent returning, Christ will then carry this rule from Heaven to earth. As such, Christ will reign with the authority and power of God and of heaven.

What Does it Mean to 'Seek First the Kingdom of God'? A verse I strongly recommend that every Christian should commit to memory and applied is Matthew 6:33: "But seek first the kingdom of God and His righteousness, and all these things shall be added to you."

Jesus taught us to pray, "Your kingdom comes. You will be done on earth as it is in heaven" (Matthew 6:10). This is praying for a day when God will bring heaven to earth and bring His rule on this planet. God still has a plan for planet Earth. He will rule and reign here, and as believers, we will rule and reign with Him. So that is in the future.

When we pray and seek the Kingdom of God, we also pray for the rule and reign of the Kingdom of God in our lives. This is when Jesus is in charge. On one occasion, Jesus said, "For indeed, the kingdom of God is within you" (Luke 17:21), where He spoke of himself. When you are under His lordship, and when He is in control of your life, that is the kingdom of God. It is not rules and regulations but "righteousness and peace and joy in the Holy Spirit" (Romans 14:17).

Seeking first the Kingdom of God also means prioritizing God's values and principles in every aspect of our lives. It involves making decisions that align with God's will, cultivating spiritual disciplines such as prayer, study of the Scriptures, and active participation in the Christian community. When we truly seek His Kingdom first, we trust that God will provide for our physical needs, just as He cares for the lilies of the field and the birds of the air (Matthew 6:26-30). This trust in God's provision frees us from anxiety and allows us to live a life characterized by peace, joy, and righteousness.

You can seek first the Kingdom of God by starting your day with morning prayers to ask for God's guidance and protection each day. People enter the Christian church through baptism, which is a symbolic death and resurrection of joining into a life with Christ as your Savior. Learn more about the proof and significance of the Resurrection of Jesus Christ here.

What Does 'Thy Kingdom Come' Have to Do with the Kingdom of God?

"This, then, is how you should pray:
"Our Father in heaven, hallowed be your name, your kingdom come, your will be done, on earth as it is in heaven. Give us today our daily bread. And forgive us our debts, as we also have forgiven our debtors. And lead us not into temptation but deliver us from the evil one."
(Matthew 6:9-13)

In what is commonly referred to as the "Lord's Prayer," we are taught to pray not only for God's will to take control of our lives but also for the saving Gospel to spread throughout the earth. We have become a part of God's kingdom when we accept the sacrifice of Jesus Christ and repent. We are then called to be witnesses of Jesus, to tell others about Him, and to remain surrendered to His will for our lives.

The phrase "Thy Kingdom come" reflects a deep longing for God's ultimate reign and the establishment of His justice and peace across the earth. This prayer acknowledges that while God's Kingdom has already been inaugurated through Jesus, its full realization is yet to come. By praying "Thy Kingdom come," Christians express their hope and anticipation for the future, when Christ will return and restore all things. It is also a commitment to live in a way that reflects Kingdom values now, as we await its full manifestation.

Praying for God's Kingdom should be our focus as Christians— for a fruitful life and for Jesus to be made known across the earth.

Jesus answered him, "Truly, truly, I say to you, unless one is born again, he cannot see the kingdom of God." ~ (John 3:3)

What Does It Mean That the Kingdom of Heaven Is at Hand?

"Repent, for the kingdom of heaven is at hand." ~ (Matthew 3:2)

The Kingdom of Heaven drew near to us when God Himself came to earth as a man. This is what John means when he says, "The Kingdom of heaven is at hand." He implied that the kingdom of heaven is now available today in the Person of the King.

The Jewish religious leaders sought a physical kingdom, not a spiritual one. So, one could say that the kingdom of heaven is a reality now in the present.

The phrase "at hand" suggests immediacy and accessibility. In Jesus, the Kingdom was not only near in time but also near in relationship, as God dwelt among humanity. For believers today, this means that we can experience the Kingdom's power and presence in our daily lives through the Holy Spirit. It calls us to live in the light of the Kingdom, embracing its values of love, mercy, and justice as we interact with the world around us.

Today, Jesus Christ lives and reigns in the hearts of all believers, yet the Kingdom of Heaven will not be completely acknowledged until all evil on the planet is judged and eliminated. Christ first came to earth to live and fulfill the role of a suffering servant. One day, he will return as ruler and judge to govern over all the earth.

The individuals who come to Christ as their Savior and recognize Him as their Lord are converted into the realm, the kingdom of the Son. They have a place with Jesus now. Christians have a closer connection with Jesus than as a subject of an earthly king.

CHAPTER 12
MORE REFLECTIVE
THOUGHTS/INSIGHTS

REFLECTIVE DEVOTIONAL, WHERE ARE YOU?

Christian or Christ Follower?

READY

"Not everyone who says to me, 'Lord, Lord,' will enter the kingdom of heaven, but the one who does the will of my Father who is in heaven. On that day many will say to me, 'Lord, Lord, did we not prophesy in your name, and cast out demons in your name, and do many mighty works in your name?' And then will I declare to them, 'I never knew you; depart from me, you workers of lawlessness.'" (Matthew 7:21-23)

SET

The stadium was filled with fans and spectators who had come to watch the championship game. The coaches and players were all in, having invested 100% of their time, energy, and resources. They had committed their lives to the sport. The stage was set for victory. While the spectators enjoyed watching the game, it was only the coaches and players who were playing the game that determined the outcome.

The fans could not influence the final score, only those

on the field.

There is a big difference between a spectator and a player or coach. In Kyle Idleman's book, Not A Fan, he distinguishes between a fan and a follower of Jesus Christ. It's easy to be a Christian. Jesus died for our sins, and we have the gift of salvation. One might say it cost us nothing. Ephesians 2:8-9 says, "For by grace you have been saved through faith; and that not of yourselves, it is the gift of God; not as a result of works, so that no one may boast."

There is a distinction between being a Christian and a Christ follower. There is a big difference between having religion and having a personal relationship with Jesus Christ. Many who call themselves Christians may have walked an aisle, said a prayer, read their Bible, listened to worship music, and perhaps been brought up in a Christian home, but are they Christ followers? Being a Christ follower comes at a great cost.

First, it cost Jesus His life! "But God demonstrates His own love toward us, in that while we were yet sinners, Christ died for us" (Romans 5:8). Jesus, perfect and sinless, died a brutal death on the cross for our sins.

Isaiah 53:5 says, "But He was pierced through for our transgressions, He was crushed for our iniquities; The chastening for our well-being fell upon Him, And by His scourging we are healed.

Second, there is a cost to the Christ follower who is 100% committed to walking in obedience to God's Word every day. They have fully surrendered their lives to Christ. Their daily priority and purpose are focused on God and His plan. They are willing to sacrifice their time, talent, and treasure for God's Kingdom work. They are in the game, on the field, or following the Coach's instructions. They are not in the stands looking on. They are actively engaged, looking to bring glory to God in every play they make in their sport and in life.

Following Jesus means He will make you a fisher of people. That involves both evangelism and discipleship. Being a Christ follower means being always prepared to share your faith and help others grow in theirs. It requires recognizing and listening to God's voice and acting on what He says. It entails constant self-denial, humility, and passionately pursuing Jesus Christ. All the disciples left everything behind to follow Jesus!

Even when counting the cost, Christ followers will be blessed beyond measure and used powerfully by God for His Kingdom work.

GO

Reflect on the difference between being a Christian as defined by the world and a Christ follower as defined by the Word.

What areas of your life do you need to surrender to Christ, to leave behind, to follow Him?

What ways can you become more of a follower of Jesus than a fan?

WORKOUT

Luke 9:23; Matthew 4:18-20; Luke 5:27; 1 Peter 2:21; John 10:27

OVERTIME

"Father, forgive me for the times that I get off track in following You. Thank You for bringing me back and keeping me on track by the power of Your Holy Spirit. Give me the wisdom and strength to fully surrender my life to You daily so that I may follow You steadfastly."

CHAPTER 13
JESUS CHRIST AND THE HOLY CROSS.

How the cross became Christianity's most popular symbol.

Throughout the world, images of the cross adorn the walls and steeples of churches. For some Christians, the cross is part of their daily attire worn around their necks. Sometimes the cross even adorns the body of a Christian in permanent ink. In Egypt, among other countries, for example, Christians wear a tattoo of the cross on their wrists. And for some Christians, each year during the beginning of Lent, they receive the cross on their foreheads in ash.

Clearly, today the cross is accepted as the most popular symbol of Christianity. But interestingly, most scholars believe that early Christians did not use the cross as an image of their religion because crucifixion evoked the shameful death of a slave or criminal.

1.Scholars believe that the first surviving public image of Jesus's crucifixion was on the fifth-century wooden doors of the Basilica of Santa Sabina, which is located on the Aventine Hill in Rome.2 Since it took approximately 400 years for Jesus's crucifixion to become an acceptable public image, scholars have traditionally believed that this means the cross did not originally function as a symbol for Christians.

crucixion-santa-sabina

Jesus and the cross: Jesus's crucifixion is displayed on

the fifth century C.E. wooden doors of the Basilica of Santa Sabina in Rome.

So how, then, did the cross become the preeminent symbol of Christianity?

The Cross in the Roman World

The word "cross" was offensive to Romans. One Roman insulted another by using it on a graffito discovered in the Stabian baths of Pompeii: "May you be nailed to the cross!" Classical texts similarly use the term "cross" in curses. The Roman writer Plautus, for instance, uses the phrase "go to an evil cross" as slang for "go to hell" (e.g., Pseudolus 331).4 In fact, even the Latin word for cross (crux) sounded harsh to the ears, according to St. Augustine (De Dialectica 10.10).

In 70 B.C.E., Cicero accused a former governor of Sicily named Gaius Verres of crucifying a Roman citizen. According to Verres, the Roman citizen named P. Gavius was guilty of espionage. Cicero reports that while Gavius was flogged in the marketplace, the only sounds from his lips were the words, "I am a Roman citizen." Despite his claim of Roman citizenship, a cross was prepared for him. "Yes, a cross," says Cicero, was prepared for this "broken sufferer, who had never seen such an accursed thing till then" (Against Verres 2.5.162).5 Worst of all, Verres ordered for Gavius to be crucified on the shore facing the Italian mainland since he claimed Roman citizenship. This incident recorded in Cicero's speech against Verres reveals that, at least for Roman elites, crucifixion was extremely rare to witness or suffer.

Unlike the Roman elites, slaves and members of the lower class were unfortunately very familiar with the cross.

The Romans primarily reserved crucifixion for

criminals and rebellious foreigners. The first-century Jewish historian Josephus records numerous instances when the Romans crucified fractious Jews in Palestine (e.g., Wars of the Jews 2.75). Of course, when the Romans crucified rebels and criminals, the cross was more than a penalty; it was also a deterrent. For instance, the Romans crucified Spartacus and his rebellious slaves on the Appian Way for everyone to see from Capua to Rome (Appian, The Civil Wars 1.120). A long row of crosses with rebellious slaves fastened to them must have discouraged other slaves from similarly revolting against their masters.

As the most extreme penalty in the Roman world, a person could suffer crucifixion in several ways. Seneca recalls seeing victims with their head down to the ground, others who had their private parts impaled, and still others with outstretched arms (De Consolatione ad Marciam 6.20.3).

When not impaled, the condemned person usually carried the horizontal beam called the patibulum to the place of execution outside the city walls. Either a soldier or public executor fastened the condemned person who was naked or wearing a loincloth to the cross with ropes or nails. Material evidence suggests that a person's feet were nailed separately on each side of the vertical beam of the cross. A crucifixion image discovered in Puteoli, Italy, for instance, shows a man, who had been severely flogged, with outstretched arms and feet nailed separately to the vertical beam.

crucifixion-puteoli

The crucifixion image from Puteoli, Italy. An ankle bone pierced with a nail found at Givat ha-Mivtar likewise attests to the practice of using one nail per foot.6 Finally, after the humiliating procession to the place of execution and the preparations for crucifixion were completed, the Romans raised the cross high in the air, so as to allow people to see the condemned person die from a long distance.

7.yehohanan-crucified-foot

To die on the cross was not only humiliating, but a slow and agonizing experience—sometimes lasting days. St. Augustine suggests that the purpose of crucifixion was to inflict as much pain as possible while prolonging death (Tractate 36.4 [John 8:15–18]). Of course, in order to maximize the amount of pain inflicted on an individual, the Romans typically tortured the victim before fastening them to the cross. While medical theories traditionally assert that people died on the cross from asphyxia (respiratory failure), recent studies contend that the victims most likely died because of a variety of physiological factors. Regardless of the actual cause of death, crucifixion was a slow and excruciatingly painful death. Christians and the Cross in the First Century.

Each of the Synoptic Gospel's recounts that now of Jesus's deepest agony as he hung on the cross, the soldiers and people in the crowd mocked him, saying, "Save yourself, and come down from the cross!" (Mark 15:30; Matthew 27:40–44; Luke 23:37–39). This sarcastic insult may certainly reflect the attitude of Jewish and Greco-Roman audiences when they first heard Paul and other early Christians preach in the first century. Simply put, their message about a crucified messiah and son of God who did not have the power to save himself from the cross seemed offensive to the Jews and foolish to Greeks and Romans (1 Corinthians 1:23).

Although the very word "cross" was so repulsive that Cicero and other Roman elites wanted nothing to do with it, each of the Gospel writers recounts Jesus's crucifixion with astonishing detail. Jesus's death on the cross, according to Mark, is not only necessary but an example of the service required for true discipleship (8:34–38). Similarly, Jesus's death on the cross is not portrayed as being shameful or humiliating in John's Gospel; there Jesus's crucifixion is envisioned as a saving event foreshadowed by Moses when he lifted the serpent in the wilderness (John 3:14).

Despite its negative connotation to Jews, Greeks, and Romans, Paul repeatedly uses the word "cross" in his letters when responding to the conflicts created by his opponents (e.g., Galatians 2:18–20). Interestingly, Paul may have deliberately focused on the modality of Jesus's death on the cross for at least two reasons. First, Paul most likely knew that, although his message about the cross was not going to easily appeal to his Jewish and Greco-Roman audiences, still it would certainly attract their attention. And second, the Jewish and Gentile criticism of Jesus's crucifixion may have encouraged Paul to focus even more of his attention on this gruesome subject since he believed Jesus demonstrated his selflessness, humility, and abundant love for humanity by suffering on the cross.

By the end of the first century, some Christians already may have viewed the cross as a significant symbol. For example, in the last decade of the first century, the author of the Book of Revelation may have referred to the mark of the cross in the seal that the servants of God receive on their foreheads (Revelation 7:2–3). Thus, the Book of Revelation possibly refers to the cross as a Christological identity marker.

Christians and the Cross in the Second and Third Centuries Greek and Roman elites continued to criticize

Christians because of their veneration of the crucified Jesus in the second century. Perhaps the most explicit criticism came from the second-century Greek philosopher Celsus, who called the way Jesus died "the most humiliating of circumstances.

It was common knowledge in the second and third centuries—even among the poorer classes of the Roman Empire—that the founder of the Christian movement suffered the most shameful death as suggested by the well-known Palatine graffito discovered in the imperial training school for slaves in Rome in 1857. This graffito depicts a donkey's hands nailed to the horizontal beam of a cross. A person beneath the cross, who is dressed like a slave in a short-sleeved shirt that extends from the shoulder to a little below the waist, gazes upward at the crucified victim in adoration as suggested by the inscription: "Alexamenos, worships god." Most likely, although it is not certain, the context of this graffito is one slave mocking another for worshiping the crucified Jesus. The inspiration for this satirical image of Jesus's crucifixion may trace back to the Greek and Latin authors who accused Christians, like the Jews, of worshiping a donkey.10 In any case, the graffito indicates that even the poorer social classes criticized the Christian belief in the crucified Jesus with sarcastic enjoyment.

alexamenos-graffito

The so-called Alexamenos graffito.

Although the image of Jesus on the cross was not very popular in the second and third centuries, still scholars have identified at least a few instances in which Christians depicted it. Perhaps the earliest portrayal of the cross by Christians occurred in the iconography of their papyrus manuscripts, specifically the Staurogram, or shape of the cross made by the overlapping of the Greek letters "Rho" and "Tau".11

A more obvious depiction of the cross is seen in a third-century gem in the British Museum, which depicts a crucified Jesus with an inscription that lists various Egyptian magical words. Furthermore, some Christians continued to mark their forehead with the image of the cross in the second and third centuries as an identity marker (e.g., Revelation 7:2–3; cf. Tertullian, On Crowns 3).12 Moreover, some scholars argue that the depiction of figures with outstretched arms in early Christian artwork may be the archetype representation of Jesus on the cross.13 Such a theory is supported by second- and third-century Christian texts, which mention Christians (especially martyrs) making the sign of the cross by stretching out their arms .

During the second and third centuries, Christians were aware that the cross was still what Paul calls a "stumbling block for the Jews and foolishness for Greeks and Romans" (1 Corinthians 1:23), and most Christians were reluctant to depict it. Nevertheless, the rhetoric of the Christian apologists, such as Justin the Martyr and Tertullian, may have encouraged at least some Christians to illustrate the cross in their art and iconography. Thus, by the end of the third century, what had once been universally a repulsive image in the ancient Mediterranean world was well on its way to becoming the preeminent symbol of Christianity. Undoubtedly, though, Constantine's adoption of the cross was the most important development that resulted in it becoming the preeminent symbol of Christianity.

According to Eusebius, the day before the Battle of Melvian Bridge, Constantine earnestly prayed for victory against his co-emperor Maxentius. Constantine's prayer was answered, and a most marvelous sign appeared to him from heaven. Eusebius relates that Constantine saw a cross of light in the sky, above the sun, bearing the inscription, "Conquer by this" (Life of Constantine 28). That night, Eusebius reports, Jesus explained to Constantine the meaning of the vision. Constantine was directed by Jesus to create a new banner with the symbol of the cross created by the Greek letters "Chi" and "Rho." This well-known symbol in Christianity, which is usually referred to as the Chi-Rho (), became known as the standard of the cross. According to the fifth-century Christian historian Sozomen, Constantine abolished crucifixion in special reverence for the power and victory he received because of the symbol of the cross (History of the Church 1.8). This abolishment certainly changed the Roman perception of the cross. Simply put, Constantine's public endorsement of the cross changed its connotation from a repulsive device for executing slaves, foreigners, and Roman citizens of low social standing into a revered, public symbol.

Constantine did not create the symbol of the cross. Rather he adopted it as a new symbol for his empire that had converted to Christianity. Of course, this means that when the artisans depicted the crucified Jesus on the wooden doors of Santa Sabina in the fifth century, the cross was no longer an offensive image. Rather the image of the cross had already transformed from an execution device to a symbol of Christianity. And soon the image of the crucifix would adorn the walls and steeples of churches throughout the world, making the cross the preeminent symbol of Christianity.

MORE RESULTS/REVELATIONS.

"And knew her not till she had brought forth her firstborn son: and he called his name JESUS."
(Matthew 1: 25)

Our Focal Scripture speaks of the firstborn son of Mary. That means, after the firstborn son, Mary went on to have more children. What looked like a great result that came first was not her last result. More results were waiting in the future. More results came her way in a matter of time. More results were appointed to her in a matter of time. She moved from result to more results. The doors of more results were open to her.

Friend, hear me as I hear the Lord: you will move from results to more results. Whatever the Lord has granted you is not the last that will come your way. Whatever doors the Lord has opened to you will not be the last He will open. Whatever change that God has brought your way will not be the last He will bring. Whatever the Lord has made happen for you will not be the last He will make happen. There is more to come.

Hear me as I hear the Lord: the doors of major results shall remain open to you. The doors of more increase shall remain open to you. The doors of more wealth shall remain open to you. The doors of more congratulations shall remain open to you. The doors of more signs and wonders shall remain open to you. The doors of more miracles shall remain open to you. The doors of more results are open to you.

I pray for you to have a much enriching better tomorrow than what you got yesterday. Seek JESUS for moment for moment advancements and never/ decline or retreat.

Rather, it will never be said that you began with results and ended empty handed. It will never be said that you began with good news and ended with nothing to show for it. It will never be said that God began with you and abandoned you on the way. It will never be said that your results became the end of results in your life. It will never be said that you moved from major results to no results.

Welcome to that season where results will make way for more results. Welcome to your season of more results. Ephesians 3: 20 (TPT) says: "Never doubt God's mighty power to work in you and accomplish all this. He will achieve infinitely more than your greatest request, your most unbelievable dream, and exceed your wildest imagination! He will outdo them all, for his miraculous power constantly energizes you."

Declare With Me: I move from results to more results, in Jesus' name!

Amen. Hallelujah.

CHAPTER 14
YOU CANNOT BE STOPPED.

"Now when Jesus was born in Bethlehem of Judaea in the days of Herod the king, behold, there came wise men from the east to Jerusalem," (Matthew 2: 1)

Our Focal Scripture speaks of how Jesus was born in Bethlehem of Judah, in the days of Herod the King. Herod was a wicked king that ruled over Israel. Herod belonged to a wicked dynasty. His reign was a reign of terror, but it didn't stop the birth of Jesus. His reign was the beginning of bitter tears for some families, but it didn't stop the emergence of Jesus. His reign was not the right time for anyone to emerge, but Jesus emerged.

Friend, hear me as I hear the Lord: no matter the number of Herods that sit on the throne—you will emerge. No matter the Herods that hold sway in the marketplace, you will still break forth on all sides. No matter the Herods that want to stand in the way of your rising, you will still rise and rise and rise. No matter the Herods that say no one will emerge under their watch, you will still emerge. No Herod will stop you from emerging.

Herod was still presiding over the affairs of the kingdom of Israel; he was in charge; he was the wrong man on the throne; he was the wrong option for anyone desiring to rise, but under his reign, Jesus came forth. Hear me as I hear the Lord: even if the Herod's of this world are sitting on the throne of the kingdom where you live, as surely as the Lord lives, you will rise.

The wrong men on the thrones of nations will not stop you.

Even if there is a Herod currently reigning in your space, you will still rise, you will still move forward; you will still make the difference you seek to make; you will still hit those important milestones you wish to hit; you will still become all that God destined you to become; you will still rise higher; you will still accomplish all that heaven destined you to accomplish; you will still make your mark in the race of destiny. You will still rise.

Welcome to that season where the reign of Herod's will not stop you from emerging. Welcome to that season where no evil on the throne will stop your rising.

Psalm 18: 29 says: "For by thee I have run through a troop; and by my God have I leaped over a wall."

Declare With Me: No Herod will stop my rising and emergence, in Jesus' Name!

CHAPTER 15
WALK IN DOMINION.

"Now when Jesus was born in Bethlehem of Judaea in the days of Herod the king, behold, there came wise men from the east to Jerusalem," (Matthew 2: 1)

Our Focal Scripture makes mention of how Herod reigned over Judah. According to Bible History, the lineage of Herod came from Edom. The family of Herod came from Edom to rule over people in Israel. Notice that God had said concerning Esau (Edom) and Jacob (Israel), that the older (Esau) will serve the younger (see Genesis 25 vs. 23). Several years later, the children of Israel became servants and subjects under sons of Esau (Edom).

Friend, hear me as I hear the Lord: whatsoever God has empowered you to rule over, will not turn around and rule over you. Whatsoever the Lord has given to be under your dominion, will not dominate over you. Whatsoever God has put under you will not arise and preside over you. No Herod will reign over you. No wicked man will rule over you. No wicked system will gain control over you. No negativity will gain control over you.

Hear me as I hear the Lord: no sickness will rule over you. No affliction from the enemy will rule over you. No conspiracy of the wicked will rules over you. No negativity that heaven did not author, will rule over you. No plan of the enemy will rule over you. No negative pattern will rule over you.

No satanic idea will rule over you. No arrow of the

enemy will rule over you. No arrangement from the pit of hell will prevail over you.

Today, I decree that you rule during your enemies. You rule over the conspiracies of the enemies of your destiny. You rule over the gates of hell. You bear rule over and above the shenanigans of men. You bear rule over the evil plots and plans against you that are yet to materialize. You rule over the policies and timelines of men. You rule over your environment. You rule over everything that the enemy may ever use against you.

Remember, you were not wired to be ruled by what God already empowered you to rule over. You will not be under the subjection of what you should dominate.

Isaiah 14: 2 GNB says: "Many nations will help the people of Israel return to the land which the LORD gave them, and there the nations will serve Israel as slaves. Those who once captured Israel will now be captured by Israel, and the people of Israel will rule over those who once oppressed them."

Declare With Me: I will not be ruled by what God has empowered me to rule, in Jesus' name!

Amen. Hallelujah.

CHAPTER 16
IT SHALL COME TO PASS.

"Now all this was done, that it might be fulfilled which was spoken of the Lord by the prophet, saying,"
(Matthew 1: 22)

Our Focal Scripture speaks of how the birth of Jesus was a fulfillment of prophecy. God gave a word, and several generations later, He was faithful to complete and fulfill what He said. The word of the Lord did not fall to the ground. The promise of God did not go without fulfillment. God knew exactly what to do to make His word a reality, and He put Joseph and Mary in the center of the fulfillment of prophecy.

Friend, hear me as I hear the Lord: you will be in the center of the fulfillment of the word of the Lord. As God decides to make His word become reality, you will be at the center of it. As God decides to fulfill His promises, you will be a beneficiary. As God chooses to cause His goodness to find expression, your life will be an example of how He manifested His goodness. As God releases His word, you will be during the fulfillment of it.

Some people merely heard about the prophecy, others saw the fulfillment, but Joseph and Mary became the channels and beneficiaries of the fulfillment of the word of the Lord. Hear me as I hear the Lord: you will not be a spectator as El Roi fulfills His word; you will be a partaker.

As others speak of what the Lord has done, you will be

the example of what the Lord has done. You will be in the center of the works of the Lord.

The season of being a mere spectator as the works of the Lord are made manifest around you, are over. The days of watching the works of God without being a partaker, are over. The days of hearing what God said without seeing same happen in your life, are over. Is there a word that God spoke to you, and you have been waiting all year for it to be fulfilled? Get set: the time for the fulfillment of the word of the Lord, is now.

Welcome to that season where the word of the Lord will come to pass in your life. Welcome to that season where heaven will put you in the center of the fulfillment of the word of the Lord.

Jeremiah 1: 12 says: "Then said the LORD unto me, thou hast well seen: for I will hasten my word to perform it."

Declare With Me: I am in the center of the fulfilment of the word of the Lord, in Jesus' name!

Amen. Hallelujah.

CHAPTER 17
TRUST AND OBEY.

"Then Joseph being raised from sleep did as the angel of the Lord had bidden him, and took unto him his wife:" (Matthew 1: 24)

Our Focal Scripture speaks of how Joseph rose from his sleep and did as the Angel of the Lord had told him to do. Joseph got a revelation from God and that first revelation was about compliance to divine instruction. In Matthew 2, God revealed to Joseph to take the child (Jesus) and His mother and run to Egypt because Herod was against them. The second instruction was about safety. Joseph obeyed the first divine instruction, and he got a second instruction about safety.

Friend, if you fail to obey the first instructions God gave you, how will He give you instructions for your safety? If you fail to obey God in matters that are not very 'serious', how will He speak to you about weightier matters? If you fail to develop a culture of obedience to God in matters that are not big, how will He freely instruct you in major destiny matters? If you fail to adapt to divine direction when the stakes are not high, how will you get divine direction when the stakes become high?

Normalize doing the right thing with God no matter how little the stakes are. Normalize obeying God in small matters. Normalize obeying God in matters that are not enough to wreak any havoc in your life. Normalize obeying divine instruction even when you seem able to do without it. Normalize obedience to divine instruction even when you do not have much to lose. Normalize obedience to God even when it seems too insignificant.

The same God who instructed Joseph by divine revelation in Matthew 1, also showed up to save him by divine revelation in Matthew 2. Put differently, obedience to divine instruction made way for more divine instruction that saved Joseph and his generation. Your obedience to current divine instructions will open the door for future divine instructions. Your obedience to God in small matters is an indication that you will obey in big issues.

Don't make the mistake of disobeying God in small matters and expect Him to show up to direct you in big matters. Don't disobey God in insignificant matters and expect Him to save you by divine revelation.

Isaiah 1: 19 says: "If ye be willing and obedient, ye shall eat the good of the land:"

Declare With Me: I choose obedience to divine instruction, in Jesus' name!

Amen. Hallelujah.

CHAPTER 18
THE ANNUAL DECEMBER 25 CHRISTMAS DAY SHOULD NEVER BE A CELEBRATION ONCE IN A YEAR. WHY AND SO WHAT?

ISAIAH 9:6 IS ALWAYS AND SHOULD GO BEYOND CHRISTMAS DAY. ISAIAH 9: 6 OUGHT TO BE A DAILY ENCOUNTER FOR THE BELIEVER.

Every year, the last one month before December 25, is considered Advent. Each of the four Sundays before Christmas represents a new week of Advent. These weeks focus on the themes of hope, joy, love, and peace as we celebrate the already (Jesus coming as a baby) and the not yet (His return to make all things right and restored).

As you and I anticipate Christmas celebrations, let us use this Isaiah 9: 6 Advent Study to unpack four names of Jesus. Each week will offer four Holy Scripture messages as well as reflection questions. Read and reflect on them all at once or throughout the week. Notice how you connect with these names and how they help you grow in your relationship with Jesus. Invite your family, neighbors, and friends to join you as you journey toward celebrations.

♣WEEK ONE IN ISAIAH 9:6.-WONDERFUL COUNSELOR.

JESUS' name - Wonderful Counselor - reflect how God

is full of wonders to a vast degree. JESUS also draws HIS people in close to guide and advise them according to HIS will and purpose.

• STUDY: Psalms 77. How do remembering God's wonders change this Psalmist perspective?

• STUDY: Hebrews 4:14-16. The Word often translated as " great" as in in " great high priest" is similar to the word " wonderful" in the original language. How have you experienced God's wonders and empathy? Discuss these moments with GOD.

• STUDY: 1 Chronicles 13: 1- 4. David sought counsel from the officers in his alarm about their next steps. What do you need to unload onto your Wonderful Counselor and seek His Wisdom and strategy about?

STUDY: Psalms 16: 7 Use this Holy Scripture as a prayer and notice how it stirs hope in you when life feels heavy and dark.

♣ WEEK TWO IN ISAIAH 9: 6- "MIGHTY GOD"

• STUDY: 1 Samuel 16 : 18.David is described as both a shepherd and a mighty warrior .When you consider JESUS as your Great Shepherd how do you depict Him as a mighty warrior (For more insights, read Psalm 23).

____

____

____

• STUDY: Psalms 45.

This Psalms was written for a historic king (possibly Solomon) but it is also seem as a prophecy about Christ and the Church. Notice in verses three and four how the king is depicted. How does this stir joy in your heart as you anticipate Jesus' return as King?

____

____

____

____

•STUDY: Romans 8: 31- 37. Consider obstacles in your life. How does knowing " God is for you' change the way you think about yourself and your circumstances?

•STUDY: 2 Corinthians 2: 14- 17. Talk with God about vivid Holy Scripture describing our victory parade in Christ and joy for Christ' s return.

____

____

♣ WEEK THREE IN ISAIAH 9: 6- " EVERLASTING FATHER"

The name of JESUS reflects how God is an eternal Father and how through Christ we are adopted as His children John 14: 6. He is not a Father who is distant, but one who is near even closer than your very breath. He is loving and full of compassion.

•STUDY: Psalms 48: 14.

As you consider your life , what else can you say will be with you forever and ever? Praise God for His infinite consistency.

____

____

____

•STUDY: Luke 11: 1- 13

What is like to connect with God as a father? Ask God to bring to mind ways He had fathered you thus far.

____

____

____

____

• STUDY: Isaiah 64: 8

How have you been shaped and molded by a biological father, mother or adopted parents, etc. God is molding and shaping in your life.

____

____

____

____

• STUDY : John 3: 16- 17 and Romans 8: 38 - 39.
Allow these truths to saturate your discussions with God as your Eternal Father full of grace and love.

____

____

____

____

WEEK FOUR IN ISAIAH 9: 6 - PRINCE OF PEACE.
The name of Jesus reflects how God is the Source of true peace and a reminder of Christ's role in bringing full restoration and peace to this world when He returns.

•STUDY: Psalms 4:8 How does God's peace impact this psalmist at night?

____

____

____

•STUDY: Revelation 1: 5- 6
How does the Apostle John use this greeting to describe the grace and peace of Jesus?

____

____

____

•STUDY: John 14: 27- 28. What did Jesus share with His followers?

____

____

●STUDY: Isaiah 52: 7

Pray the fullness of Good News as described in this Holy Scriptures over family, neighbors, friends, community city, village, state, country and the globe.

REFLECTIONS OF JESUS IN MINISTRY

Baptism with those that are saved.

Rejoicing After Baptism.

Prepared and Ready for Missions.

CHM: Reaching/Meeting the Children where they are.

Little ones/parents Hungry for the Word of God.

Rejoicing in the Lord at the CHM Strategic Leadership Conference in the Republic of Mali.

Key Leadership Conference at Theological Seminary, Ndu, Cameroon, Central Africa.

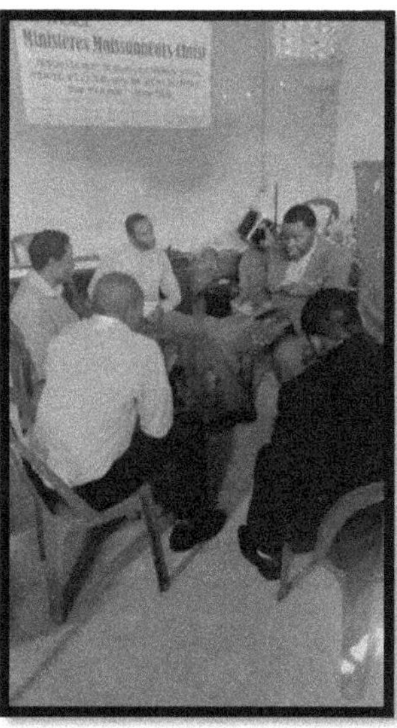

(L) Dr. Finn. CHM at the entrance of the Theological Seminary Audotoruim, with Dr.Nobia the Host who also had PhD.in Nuclear Physics. Professor in the US.

(R) CHM President in DRC, Kinshasa strategically working on evangelism with core leaders.

**Senior Pastors/ Ministers/Leaders at the
Central Africa Key Conference.**

**In rapt attention Senior Pastors/Ministers/Leaders at the
Ndu, Cameroon Key Conference.**

Vessels of God further equipped at the Conference through CHM.

Vessels— men/women receiving His Word at the Conference.

Dad, Mom, and daughter with the CHM President.

Beautiful/blessed family of our Senior Pastor in the South of the Sahara.

**Dr. & Dr. Mrs. Dayo
Opadeyi, CHM Board Trustees.**

CHM ministering along with Dr Apiagu.

The young couple ready for the Call.

**Papa Rev. John Adeoye, Chairman CHM Trustees Board
receiving a plague of appreciation.**

Dedication of His servant in CHM.

More souls dedicated to the move of the Holy Spirit.

More Jesus and less of me!

CHM Precious woman of God that carries the mantle of the ladies/women in-reaches/out reaches.

CHM North of America ladies/women with Rev. Mrs. Elizabeth Adenowo at the extreme left standing. Her husband Rev. Segun Adenowo at the back row with the CHM President.

Mama, and Evangelist Fabiyi with the CHM President.

Rev. Segun Adenowo and our precious Minister.

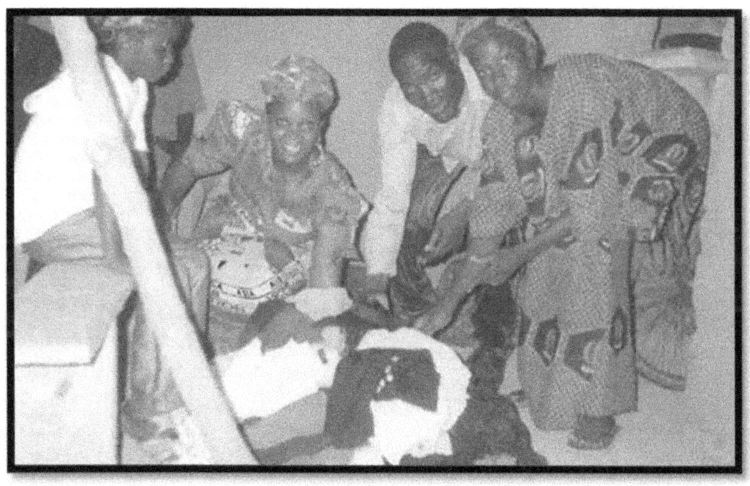

**Some kind of physical/materials support.
Brethren carefully sorting out stuff.**

Ongoing CHM Elementary School Project.

No child should be left behind.CHM work in progress.

Pouring out as brethren allowed the Holy Spirit to do His work in our midst.

Lifting JESUS in DRC.
The young are growing. Dedicated CHM Educators willing to take extra mile.

Willingness to share with each other.

**CHM, DRC addressing the Church
and by side is the Missionary Pastor.**

**Outreach flyer in Central Africa.
Meeting people were they are.**

CHM Key Leaders -Seeking to share and plan ahead.

**Here we go- Ashes for Beauty. CHM School Children
from the hidden village in one
of the West African countries.**

Here we go again.

Quality Education from CHM.

Christ centered teachers transforming lives.

**CHM Health is Wealth Annual Outreach
in Sierra Leone.**

Attentiveness to the Word.- Mother and Child.

New life in Christ.

CHM TRUSTES - Awards of Doctorates degree to veteran Pastors Leroy & Anna Tolliver, California USA.

CHM President with Wife Co-Founder, and their daughter.

Adoring/ Decorating the Tolivers.

**Presentation of the Doctorate of Ministry
to Dr. Leroy Toliver.**

**Congratulations to
Dr. & Dr. Leroy & Anna Toliver.**

Adoring/ Decorating the Tolivers

There comes Pastor Anna Toliver being blessed/decorated /honored with the Doctorate degree in Ministry.

The Toliver's Children joined with their parents with the celebrations.